BOOKS BY F. SCOTT FITZGERALD

SCOTT FITZGERALD

Letters to His Daughter

SCOTT FITZGERALD:

Letters to His Daughter.

EDITED BY ANDREW TURNBULL,

WITH AN INTRODUCTION
BY
Frances Fitzgerald Lanahan

CHARLES SCRIBNER'S SONS, *NEW YORK*

INTRODUCTION

INTRODUCTION

In my next incarnation, I may not choose again to be the daughter of a Famous Author. The pay is good, and there are fringe benefits, but the working conditions are too hazardous. People who live entirely by the fertility of their imaginations are fascinating, brilliant, and often charming, but they should be sat next to at dinner parties, not lived with. Imagine depending for your happiness upon a Bernard Shaw or a Somerset Maugham, not to mention such contemporary stars as Norman Mailer! I have the impression that the only people quite as insufferable as writers are painters.

I have much puzzled over the why of this, and have compiled a few tentative answers. First, I suppose it is impossible to form the habit of inventing people, building them up, tearing them down, and moving them around like paper dolls, without doing somewhat the same thing with live ones. Good writers are essentially muckrakers, exposing the scandalous condition of the human soul. It is their job to strip veneers from situations and personalities. The rest of us accept our fellow beings at face value, and swallow what we can't accept. Writers can't: they have to prod, poke, question, test, doubt, and challenge, which requires a constant flow of fresh victims and fresh experience.

Second, there is nothing anybody else can do to help a writer. A company president can take on an executive assistant; a lawyer can hire a clerk; even a housewife can unload up to seventy or eighty per cent of her duties. The poor writer can turn to no one but himself until his work is finished, when he can take it to an editor who will show him how to start all over, by himself.

He can never say, "Here, Mary—you know this subject as well as I do—be a dear and finish this paragraph for me, will you?"

Third, successful writers, like all successful people, are spoiled and indulged by everybody with whom they come in contact. They are, at the same time, spared the rod of discipline imposed by other occupations. A Senator must face the press, greet thousands of constituents, sit through vistaless Saharas of banquets without the oasis of an entertaining word or a glass of wine. An actress must turn up at the theater or the movie set, take care of her looks, memorize her lines. The poor writer is free to do whatever he chooses; if he chooses to get drunk, who can fire him? Between himself and doom stands no one but his creditor.

Revered and pampered, he must sit down at his desk each day alone, without rules or guidelines, exactly as if he had previously accomplished nothing. Small wonder he is not all sweetness and light when he emerges, often unvictoriously, from the battle.

So the fact that my father became a difficult parent does not surprise or offend me. He gave me a golden childhood, which is as much as any of us can ask for. I can remember nothing but happiness and delight in his company until the world began to be too much for him, when I was about eleven years old. But from the time the first of the letters in this collection was written, when I first went off to camp, until he died in 1940, appropriately closing the pre-World War II era as he appropriately timed his whole life to coincide with the nation's, I can remember almost nothing but the troubles which were reflected in our relations—my mother's hopeless illness, his own bad health and lack of money, and, hardest of all I think, his literary eclipse.

During the last five years of my father's life, he couldn't have bought a book of his in any bookstore; he probably couldn't even have asked for one without getting a blank stare from the saleslady. I am not sentimental by nature, but once a few years ago when I walked into the bookshop of a remote town and saw a whole shelf of F. Scott Fitzgerald sitting there as naturally as if it had been the works of Shakespeare, I burst into tears. A sick wife, poverty, bad luck—we all have to contend with some of these things, and Daddy had helped bring on a good bit of it himself. But the writing part wasn't fair; God had played one of those trump cards which can defeat even the most valiant of us.

So much has been said about him that, to paraphrase Dorothy Parker, if all the reams of paper about F. Scott Fitzgerald were stretched across the Atlantic, I wouldn't be a bit surprised. Edmund Wilson, Arthur Mizener, Sheilah Graham, Andrew Turnbull, Malcolm Cowley, Vance Bourjaily, Arnold Gingrich, Dan Piper, Matthew Bruccoli, John Kuehl, Glenway Wescott, Morley Callaghan, Burke Wilkinson, not to mention Mr. Hemingway with his piercing jabs at the prone body, or the dozens of others who have written Ph.D. theses and articles in magazines large and small, or Budd Schulberg who made a fortune with his photographic description of my father's lowest moment, have all put it far better than I could. The only thing new I can add is a little bit about me.

I was not a perspicacious teenager, and in fact was probably more self-preoccupied than most. But even I dimly perceived, even then, that my father was not only a genius but a great man in his way, despite his partly self-inflicted torments and his gigantic sins. I knew that he was kind, generous, honorable, and loyal, and I admired him and loved him. But self-preservation being the strongest instinct any of us have, especially when we are young, I also knew that there was only one way for me to survive his tragedy, and that was to ignore it. Looking back, I wish I'd been a less exasperating daughter, more thoughtful, more assiduous and more considerate. I hate knowing how much I must have added to his troubles, which is probably why I haven't written about him, in a personal way, long before this.

I was busy surviving, and what I couldn't ignore in the way of objectionable behavior, such as an inkwell flying past my ear, I would put up in the emotional attic as soon as possible. After the ghastly tea-dance, for example, the preparation for which is mentioned in these letters, my friend Peaches Finney and I went back to her house in a state of semi-hysteria. Her parents, who were about the nicest and most considerate people I've ever known, fed us eggs and consolation. Within two hours we were dressed and curled, and deposited by them at the door of the next Christmas party. Meredith Boyce, then the best sixteen-year-old dancer in Baltimore, actually stopped dancing long enough to ask me to sit down.

"How can you seem so *cheerful?*" he asked. He was a very good friend; in fact I flattered myself that we had a case of puppy love. "After what happened this afternoon?"

"Nothing happened this afternoon," I said.

"Are you being brave? Smiling through the tears?"

"Not at all. It just never happened, that's all."

He told me much later that he had been shocked by my detachment that evening. I asked him why.

"Because kids should care more about their parents," he said. "He was so drunk, and so pitiful, and you acted as if he wasn't there."

"Meredith, I *had* to," I said. "Don't you see that if I'd allowed myself to care, I couldn't have stood it?"

He was unconvinced—he probably still is—and in one way he was right. The trouble with the ostrich approach is that if you use it long enough, it becomes a habit. There are comic-strip jokes about the husband-wife situation in which neither one hears the other until somebody yells "FIRE!" I developed an immunity against my father, so that when he bawled me out for something, I simply didn't hear it.

So these gorgeous letters, these absolute pearls of wisdom and literary style, would arrive at Vassar and I'd simply examine them for checks and news, then stick them in my lower right-hand drawer. I'm proud of myself for saving them; I knew they were great letters, and my motives were certainly not acquisitive, because Daddy was an impecunious and obscure author then, with no prospect in sight of *The Great Gatsby* being translated into twenty-seven languages. I saved them the way you save *War and Peace* to read, or Florence to spend some time in later.

But at the time I didn't want to be told what to read, how to read it, what courses to take, whether to try out for the college paper, what girls to room with, what football games to go to, how to feel about the Spanish Civil War, whether or not to drink, whether or not to "throw myself away" (if only Daddy had had a daughter at Vassar *now*, what glorious prose he could have composed on this subject!), not to write music for our campus productions, not to put a peroxide streak in my hair, not to go to a debutante party in New York, whether or not to try my hand at social work, and so on and on until I half expected, at the age of eighteen, to be lectured to on when to take a bath.

The thing he disapproved of most was a weekend I never took; Andrew Turnbull asked me what I actually did —I think I went down for a surreptitious visit to the Harold Obers in Scarsdale, who were my substitute parents. There must have been twenty telegrams from California before I got back to college Sunday night.

The thing he approved of most was my going to Harvard Summer School, the year he died. It does have an intellectual-sounding ring, and I'm glad I gave him a sense of accomplishment. In all of my some forty years now, I don't think I've ever done anything so utterly, ridiculously frivolous. I met up with a group of charming people who had flunked out of Harvard for one reason or another, and had such a good time I never took the exams. I spent more time in Cambridge night clubs, wasting time, than I've ever

xiv

had a chance to do before or since. You'll be relieved to hear that Daddy never learned the full extent of what he doubtless would have considered his daughter's slothfulness and wanton preparation for a life of sin.

Malcolm Cowley said in a review in *The New York Times* once that "Fitzgerald wasn't writing those letters to his daughter at Vassar; he was writing them to himself at Princeton." This is the point, really. I was an imaginary daughter, as fictional as one of his early heroines. He made me sound far more popular and glamorous than I was— I was actually only vaguely pretty, and only danced with by friends, of which fortunately I had a number—but he wanted me so desperately to be so that in these letters, I sound like my contemporary glamor queen, Brenda Frazier. He also made me sound more wicked and hell-bent on pleasure than I could possibly have been. It's true that I preferred boys, Fred Astaire, and fun to the sheer hard labor of working. I *still* prefer boys, Fred Astaire, and fun to the sheer hard labor of working. Doesn't almost everybody?

There's a moral to all this, and I'm about to get it off my chest:

To college students (including my own two): "Don't ignore any good advice, unless it comes from your own parents. Somebody else's parents might very well be right."

To parents (poor struggling creatures): "Don't drop your pearls before swine, at least without making sure the swine are going to put them in the lower right-hand drawer."

Listen carefully to my father, now. Because what he

offers is good advice, and I'm sure if he hadn't been my own father that I loved and "hated" simultaneously, I would have profited by it and be the best educated, most attractive, most successful, most faultless woman on earth today.

—SCOTTIE LANAHAN

NOTE

It being the essence of a letter that we should have the whole of each, no cuts have been made save in passages that might offend the living, and in most cases it has been sufficient to substitute blanks for names. All omissions of words and sentences have been indicated by four dots since Fitzgerald sometimes used three dots as punctuation. In general his punctuation has been observed, except where it confuses the sense. The use of italics and quotation marks have been standardized, however (titles of books, plays, movies, magazines and newspapers in italics, titles of poems and short stories in quotes). Sometimes his memory of a book or poem title was a little off, but as the titles are easily recognizable, they have been left as he wrote them. Fitzgerald was a lamentable speller. Following his ear, he habitually made such slips as "definate" and "critisism," and proper names were his downfall. He always reversed the "ei" in "Dreiser," "Stein," and "Hergesheimer," and, despite the hundreds of times he had seen "Hemingway" in print, he wrote it either "Hemmingway" or "Hemminway" and was capable of "Earnest" for "Ernest." Those who are interested will find copious examples of boners in previous books about him; here it has seemed advisable to correct them.

—ANDREW TURNBULL

CONTENTS

SCOTT FITZGERALD

Letters to His Daughter

La Paix, Rodgers' Forge
Towson, Maryland

AUGUST 8, 1933

Dear Pie:

I feel very strongly about you doing [your] duty. Would you give me a little more documentation about your reading in French? I am glad you are happy—but I never believe much in happiness. I never believe in misery either. Those are things you see on the stage or the screen or the printed page, they never really happen to you in life.

All I believe in in life is the rewards for virtue (according to your talents) and the *punishments* for not fulfilling your duties, which are doubly costly. If there is such a volume in the camp library, will you ask Mrs. Tyson to let you look up a sonnet of Shakespeare's in which the line occurs *"Lilies that fester smell far worse than weeds."*

Have had no thoughts today, life seems composed of getting up a *Saturday Evening Post* story. I think of you, and always pleasantly; but if you call me "Pappy" again I am going to take the White Cat out and beat his bottom *hard, six times for every time you are impertinent.* Do you react to that?

I will arrange the camp bill.

Halfwit, I will conclude.

Things to worry about:
Worry about courage
Worry about cleanliness
Worry about efficiency

3

Worry about horsemanship
Worry about. . .
Things not to worry about:
Don't worry about popular opinion
Don't worry about dolls
Don't worry about the past
Don't worry about the future
Don't worry about growing up
Don't worry about anybody getting ahead of you
Don't worry about triumph
Don't worry about failure unless it comes through your own fault
Don't worry about mosquitoes
Don't worry about flies
Don't worry about insects in general
Don't worry about parents
Don't worry about boys
Don't worry about disappointments
Don't worry about pleasures
Don't worry about satisfactions
Things to think about:
What am I really aiming at?
How good am I really in comparison to my contemporaries in regard to:
(a) Scholarship
(b) Do I really understand about people and am I able to get along with them?
(c) Am I trying to make my body a useful instrument or am I neglecting it?

With dearest love,

[Daddy]

P.S. My come-back to your calling me Pappy is christening you by the word Egg, which implies that you belong to a very rudimentary state of life and that I could break you up and crack you open at my will and I think it would be a word that would hang on if I ever told it to your contemporaries. "Egg Fitzgerald." How would you like that to go through life with—"Eggie Fitzgerald" or "Bad Egg Fitzgerald" or any form that might occur to fertile minds? Try it once more and I swear to God I will hang it on you and it will be up to you to shake it off. Why borrow trouble?

Love anyhow.

Grove Park Inn
Asheville, North Carolina

[SUMMER, 1935]

Scottina:

It was fine seeing you, and I liked you a lot (this is aside from loving you which I always do). You are nicer to adults —you are emerging from that rather difficult time in girls, 12–15 usually, but you are emerging I think rather early— probably at 14 or so. You have one good crack coming but —well:

"Daddy the prophet!" I can hear you say in scorn. I wish to God I wasn't so right usually about you. When I wrote that "news-sheet" with events left out, you know— the letter that puzzled you—and headed it "Scottie Loses Head," it was because I saw it coming. I knew that your popularity with two or three dazed adolescent boys would convince you that you were at least the Queen of Sheba, and that you would "lose your head." What shape this hay-wire excursion would take I didn't know—I couldn't have guessed it would be writing a series of indiscreet letters to a gossipy and indiscreet boy who would show them to the persons for whom they were *not* meant (Understand: I don't blame Andrew [1] too much—the fault was yours—he didn't, will you notice, put into writing an analysis of his best friends of his own sex!).

However, that's of no seriousness. But I think that the next kick will be a bad one—but you will survive, and after that you will manage your affairs better. To avoid such

[1] Andrew Turnbull.

6

blows you almost *have* to have them yourself so you can begin to think of others as valuing themselves, possibly, quite as much as you do yourself. So I'm not afraid of it for you. I don't want it to be so bad that it will break your self-confidence, which is attractive and is fine [if] founded on positive virtues, work, courage, etc., but if you are selfish it had better be broken early. If you are unselfish you can keep it always—and it is a nice thing to have. I didn't know till 15 that there was anyone in the world except me, and it cost me *plenty*.

Signs and portents of your persistent conceit: Mrs. Owens [2] said to me (and Mrs. Owens loves you), "For the first time in a long while Scottie was *nice*, and not a burden as I expected. It was really nice to be with her."

Because, I guess, for the first time you entered into *their* lives, humble lives of struggling people, instead of insisting that they enter into yours—a chance they never had, of belonging to "high society." Before, you had let them be aware of what *you* were doing (not in any snobbish sense, because heaven knows I'd have checked you on that)—but because you never considered or pretended to consider their lives, their world at all—your own activities seemed of so much more overwhelming importance to you! *You did not use one bit of your mind, one little spot!* to think what *they* were thinking, or help *them!*

You went to Norfolk and gave out the information (*via* the Taylors, *via* Annabel, *via* mother) that you were going to Dobbs. That doesn't matter save as indicative of a show-off frame of mind. You know it was highly tentative. It was

[2] Mrs. Allein Owens had been Fitzgerald's secretary since May, 1932.

a case, again, of boasting, of "promoting yourself." But those signs of one big catastrophe (it'll come—I want to minimize it for you, but it can't be prevented because only experience can teach) are less important than your failure to realize that you are *a young member of the human race*, who has not proved itself in any but the most superficial manner. (I have seen "popular girls" of 15 become utterly *déclassé* in six months because they were essentially selfish.) You and Peaches [3] (who isn't selfish, I think) had a superficial head-start with prettiness, but you will find more and more that less pretty girls will be attaching the solider, more substantial boys as the next two years will show. Both you and Peaches are intelligent but both of you will be warped by this early attention, *and something tells me she won't lose her head;* she hasn't the "gift of gab" as you have—her laughter and her silence takes the place of much. That's why I wish to God you would write something when you have time—if only a one act play about how girls act in the bath house, in a tent, on a train going to camp.

I grow weary, but I probably won't write again for a month. Don't answer this, justifying yourself—of *course* I know you're doing the best you "can."

The points of the letter are:

1st   You did spill over, rashly!

2nd You are getting over the selfish period—thank God!

3d   But it'll take one more big kick, and I want it to be mild, so your backside won't suffer too much.

4th   I wish you'd get your mind off your precious self

---

[3] Peaches Finney, a close friend of Scottie's.

8

enough to write me a one act play about other people
—what they say and how they behave.

    With *dearest* love,
        Your simply so-perfect too-too
                            Daddy

Please, turn back and read this letter over! It is too packed
with considered thought to digest the first time. Like Milton
—oh yeah!

[JULY, 1935]

Darlin':

Am on a flying visit to New York. Spent yesterday afternoon with, of all people, Elissa Landi. She sailed for Europe last night. She is very nice.

I am not going to write you much this summer but you know my heart is with you always. Remember the one thing about riding—that you can't be as reckless at it as you can about swimming, because there's another factor besides yourself involved, the *horse*. So that no matter *how* good you were if the horse was bad there might be trouble. Different from diving, for example, where you have only yourself to blame. The point is, don't do anything or try anything that the riding master doesn't approve of. He knows just the point you've reached at handling the mount.

Good-by double durling. Aunt Rosalind,[1] Mr. Ober [2] and Mr. Perkins [3] all invite you to spend a few days with them in N.Y. when camp is over. We shall see. I leave for the South Monday.

Your utterly irresistible

Daddy

[1] Zelda's sister, Mrs. Newman Smith.
[2] Harold Ober, Fitzgerald's literary agent.
[3] Maxwell Perkins, Fitzgerald's editor.

[*Grove Park Inn*]
[*Asheville, North Carolina*]

AUGUST 4, 1935

Darling:

I always thought the first book of that series was one of the most exciting books I ever read.[1] Ernest Hemingway thought so too. Please read it with a view to a possible dramatization of it and tell me your opinion. I never went any further in that series than the first one on account of no English versions being available.

I am glad you fell off your horse. Here in Carolina the only conveyance is by zebra. I have one zebra named Clarence.

My correspondence is now limited to five people: Elissa Landi, Mrs. Roosevelt, Aquilla,[2] and a fourth whom I need scarcely mention, because I hardly know his name.

Darling, I am working hard and getting very well.

Please unleash yourself in your letters to your mother *without mentioning riding catastrophes* which might make her nervous.

Give my affectionate regards to Virginia, Helen [and] Betty and tell your counselor what a really obnoxious person you might turn out to be unless carefully watched.

Your stoogie—

Daddy

---

[1] An Alexander Dumas series, which one uncertain.
[2] At one time Fitzgerald's chauffeur.

Darling:

O.K. about the tutoring. Let it slide. But I hate to let one season slip by at your age without one difficult advance.

Do something for me! I'm proud of the swimming but summer's only summer. Give me a time maybe, and know always I'm thinking of you and for you, and my plans will come to you as soon as crystallized, sometime in August. Slim chance of my getting up to Pennsylvania. All Europe ideas definitely out. Spain was what I wanted to see and Spain is in what the newsmen call the "throes of revolution."

Your mother likes your letters so much. Hope you have nice tent mates. I don't agree with Mrs. Tappan on that subject, but that's a whole story and I know whatever the situation is you'll make the best of it in your own courageous way.

Oh darling Scottie—I don't want to force you but it does please me when you can make a connection between the Louisiana Purchase and why Fred Astaire lifts up his left hind foot for the world's pleasure. I want you to be among the best of your race and not waste yourself on trivial aims. To be useful and proud—is that too much to ask?

I enclose you the jacket of my latest book. I have decided to write in Scandinavian from now on!

Your devoted

Daddy

Grove Park Inn
Asheville, North Carolina

JULY 31, 1936

Darling:

I am enclosing in this some pictures that tell a sad story. I had a terrific accident and broke my shoulder. I thought I would be very smart and do some diving and after a year and a half of inactivity I stretched my muscles too much in the air and broke my shoulder. It has all been very troublesome and expensive but I have tried to be as cheerful as possible about it and everyone has been very kind; the people here have rigged up a curious writing board for me so that I work with my hand over my head rather like this.[1]

I enclose money for your present small needs. It may be that the expenses of this injury will preclude your going to an expensive school this fall but life sometimes does those things to you and I know you are brave and able to adjust yourself to changing conditions and to know that all the effort that I have will be thrown into your education and the care of your mother. If I had not had this operation on my shoulder the doctor tells me I would never have been able to raise my arm above my shoulder again. It is still an open bet as to whether or not I will ever be able to raise it above my shoulder.

I am proud of you and I am only a little angered by the fact that you have not managed to read more than one of the French books.

[1] Fitzgerald had drawn a picture of himself seated at his writing board.

Sunday night I leave for Baltimore and you can write me either there care of Mrs. Owens or here where I am returning. Isn't it lucky I did not go to Spain after all! Or maybe it would have been rather fun.

Your loving

Daddy

Dearest Scottina:

I had already decided to go up Thanksgiving which I will do, God willing, and so on your own suggestion I have killed the idea of going up on your birthday. You seem to understand the fact that I cannot afford at the moment to make two trips within the same month; so I know you won't be unduly disappointed.

To finish up news of me, the arm is really definitely out of danger and I am going to be able to use it again, which I doubted for three or four weeks. Went out to [a] football game with the Flynns last Saturday, the same sort of game exactly that we went to last fall at very much the same time. Lefty was his usual handsome self and Nora was charming as always. They asked about you repeatedly, and not because they thought they ought to but because they have a real affection for you, and I mean both of them. They were so happy to know that you are getting along so well at your school.

Confirming my Christmas plans, they are, briefly: that we shall have a party for you in Baltimore at the Belvedere or the Stafford, if we can afford it! Then the actual Christmas Day will be spent either here with your mother (it won't be like that awful Christmas in Switzerland), or else you and your mother and the trained nurse will go to Montgomery and spend Christmas with your grandmother; perhaps with a little time afterwards in Baltimore before you go back to school.

Don't be a bit discouraged about your story not being tops. At the same time, I am not going to encourage you about it, because, after all, if you want to get into the big time, you have to have your own fences to jump and learn from experience. Nobody ever became a writer just by wanting to be one. If you have anything to say, anything you feel nobody has ever said before, you have got to feel it so desperately that you will find some way to say it that nobody has ever found before, so that the thing you have to say and the way of saying it blend as one matter—as indissolubly as if they were conceived together.

Let me preach again for a moment: I mean that what you have felt and thought will, by itself, invent a new style, so that when people talk about style they are always a little astonished at the newness of it, because they think that it is only *style* that they are talking about, when what they are talking about is the attempt to express a new idea with such force that it will have the originality of the thought. It is an awfully lonesome business, and, as you know, I never wanted you to go into it, but if you are going into it at all I want you to go into it knowing the sort of things that took me years to learn.

Why are you whining about such matters as study hall, etc., when you deliberately picked this school [1] as the place you wanted to go above all places? Of course it is hard. Nothing any good isn't hard, and you know you have never been brought up soft, or are you quitting on me suddenly? Darling, you know I love you, and I expect you to live up absolutely to what I laid out for you in the beginning.

Scott

[1] Ethel Walker's.

Grove Park Inn
Asheville, North Carolina

NOVEMBER 17, 1936

Dearest Pie:

I got a School Letter saying that Thanksgiving Day is best, and it is better for me that way. There is no particular advantage in going out two or three times rather than one, without particular objectives; the idea is to go out once and have a good time. I'll be delighted to meet whoever you want, and our engagement is on Thanksgiving Day.

(This is a parenthesis: I got the little charms that you sent me for my birthday, the bells dangling and the mule, and appreciated your thought of me—you little donkey!)

Park Avenue girls are hard, aren't they? Usually the daughters of "up-and-coming" men and, in a way, the inevitable offspring of that type. It's the "Yankee push" to its last degree, a sublimation of the sort of Jay Gould who began by peddling bad buttons to a county and ended, with the same system of peddler's morals, by peddling five dollar railroads to a nation.

Don't mistake me. I think of myself always as a northerner—and I think of you the same way. Nevertheless, we are all of one nation and you will find all the lassitude and laziness there that you despise, enough to fill Savannah and Charleston, just as down here you will find the same "go getter" principle in the Carolinas.

I don't know whether you will stay there another year —it all depends on your marks and your work, and I can't give you the particular view of life that I have (which as

17

you know is a tragic one), without dulling your enthusiasm. A whole lot of people have found life a whole lot of fun. I have not found it so. But, I had a hell of a lot of fun when I was in my twenties and thirties; and I feel that it is your duty to accept the sadness, the tragedy of the world we live in, with a certain *esprit*.

Now, insofar as your course is concerned, there is no question of your dropping mathematics and taking the easiest way to go into Vassar, and being one of the girls fitted for nothing except to reflect other people without having any particular character of your own. I want you to take mathematics up to the limit of what the school offers. I want you to take physics and I want you to take chemistry. I don't care about your English courses or your French courses at present. If you don't know two languages and the ways that men chose to express their thoughts in those languages by this time, then you don't sound like my daughter. You are an only child, but that doesn't give you any right to impose on that fact.

I want you to know certain basic scientific principles, and I feel that it is impossible to learn them unless you have gone as far into mathematics as coordinate geometry. *I don't want you to give up mathematics next year*. I learned about writing from doing something that I didn't have any taste for. If you don't carry your mathematics such as coordinate geometry (conic sections), you will have strayed far afield from what I had planned for you. I don't insist on the calculus, but it is certainly nothing to be decided by what is easiest. You are going into Vassar with mathematical credits and a certain side of your life there is going to be scientific.

Honey, I wish I could see you. It would be so much

easier to go over these important matters without friction, but at a distance it seems rather tough that you are inclined to slide into the subjects that are easy for you, like modern languages.

No more until I see you Thanksgiving.

With dearest love,

F. Scott Fitz

P.S. Sorry you are on bounds—feel as if I had been the same for six months. However I have bought an ancient Packard roadster and get out more now. I always allow for your exuberance but I hope this doesn't come from a feud with any special teacher, or from any indiscretion of speech, a fault you should be beginning to control.

Dear Scottie:

As I wired you, there is no question of having ninety people. The most you can possibly ask is about sixty people; and even that is counting on ten or twelve refusals. If I had thought that the Ethel Walker School was going to give you a peculiar idea of what your financial resources are, it would have been far, far better to send you to a modest school here in the Carolina mountains. You are a poor girl, and if you don't like to think about it, just ask me. If you don't make up your mind to being that, you become one of those terrible girls that don't know whether they are millionairesses or paupers. You are neither one nor the other. The dance for you in Baltimore is a very modest one. It will have dignity because it pretends to nothing that it isn't. It will give you a certain amount of whoopee and it will probably lack a certain amount of things that you would expect. For instance, I am determined to have a hurdy-gurdy for the orchestra—you know, an Italian with a monkey, and I think the children will be very content with that. They don't want much, children of sixteen or seventeen, and they will be amused by the antics of the monkey. Your idea of a swing orchestra seems zero to me.

However, in the next room I will have some of the older people with a swing orchestra that I have engaged, and from time to time you may bring some of your choice friends in there to dance.

—But remember that I expect you and your crowd to dance by the hurdy-gurdy during the whole afternoon, quietly and slowly and without swing music, just doing simple waltz dancing.

You can stay all night all you want with people up to the night of December 24th, when you and I are going to make a hop South.

With dearest love,

Daddy

P.S. You ask what to put on the cards. It should be about like this:

MISS FRANCES SCOTT FITZGERALD

F. SCOTT FITZGERALD

December 22nd
Four to six
Hotel Belvedere   *Dancing*

Darling Scottina:

I loved having you here (except in the early morning) and I think we didn't get along *so* badly, did we? Glad you had a gay time in Baltimore and New York and have a friend at Groton. They are very democratic there—they have to sleep in gold cubicles and wash at old platinum pumps. This toughens them up so they can pay the poor starvation wages without weakening. (By the way, the older boys *only* can smoke at Andover and in a special place—you wretched liar you!)

The horse show is Wednesday. Everyone asks about you and really means it, some of them. La Sprague said her mother forgot to invite you to some party she gave and was in tears. She has two Williams boys who are here at the hotel on her trail. Caroline Kelly sends her love. I see your mother tomorrow. Finally finished my story (very good) and am starting another and a play on the side. Hollywood postponed but may come through.

What did you do in Baltimore? How were Peaches and Meredith?
Answer.

With dearest love to my slew-footed angel,

Daddy

P.S. What about the toil? Are you sweating gall and vinegar?

Dearest Pie:

What an exit! Horrors of life in the sticks—nothing could have turned around there except a model T Ford. Sorry to leave you and Grandma in such a mess.

The air trip was fine—very thrilling as always. I'm sending this to the Obers where I hope you are by now. Also by the time you get this I'll have heard from the Mac-Arthurs though I know it's all right. It will be great to have you with me in Hollywood. I know Freddie Bartholomew will love taking you around to birthday parties in the afternoons, and you'll find Shirley Temple as good a pal as Peaches and more loyal.

Where on earth did you get that preconception that I think of you as a scarlet woman? Hell, you're a romantic but that's not in your disfavor. It's all right to like affection, but not when you drive, in the immortal words of Mitzi Green. I simply don't want you in danger and I don't want you to do anything inappropriate to your age. For premature adventure one pays an atrocious price. As I told you once, every boy I know who drank at eighteen or nineteen is now safe in his grave. The girls who were what we called "speeds" (in our stone-age slang) at sixteen were reduced to anything they could get at the marrying time. It's in the logic of life that no young person ever "gets away with anything." They fool their parents but not their contemporaries. It was in the cards that Ginevra King should get fired from Westover—also that your mother should wear out young. I think that despite a tendency to self indulgence

23

you and I have some essential seriousness that will manage to preserve us. Whatever your sins are I hope you never get to justify them to yourself.

With dearest love,

Daddy

Dearest Pie:

This may be the last letter for a time, though I won't forget the check when I get at my check book.

I feel a certain excitement. The third Hollywood venture. Two failures behind me though one no fault of mine. The first one was just ten years ago. At that time I had been generally acknowledged for several years as the top American writer both seriously and, as far as prices went, popularly. I had been loafing for six months for the first time in my life and was confident to the point of conceit. Hollywood made a big fuss over us and the ladies all looked very beautiful to a man of thirty. I honestly believed that with *no effort on my part* I was a sort of magician with words—an odd delusion on my part when I had worked so desperately hard to develop a hard, colorful prose style.

Total result—a great time and no work. I was to be paid only a small amount unless they made my picture— they didn't.

The second time I went was five years ago. Life had gotten in some hard socks and while all was serene on top, with your mother apparently recovered in Montgomery, I was jittery underneath and beginning to drink more than I ought to. Far from approaching it too confidently I was far too humble. I ran afoul of a bastard named de Sano, since a suicide, and let myself be gypped out of command. I wrote the picture and he changed as I wrote. I tried to get at Thalberg but was erroneously warned against it as "bad

25

taste." Result—a bad script. I left with the money, for this was a contract for weekly payments, but disillusioned and disgusted, vowing never to go back, tho they said it wasn't my fault and asked me to stay. I wanted to get East when the contract expired to see how your mother was. This was later interpreted as "running out on them" and held against me.

(The train has left El Paso since I began this letter—hence the writing—Rocky Mountain writing.)

I want to profit by these two experiences—I must be very tactful but keep my hand on the wheel from the start —find out the key man among the bosses and the most malleable among the collaborators—then fight the rest tooth and nail until, in fact or in effect, I'm alone on the picture. That's the only way I can do my best work. Given a break I can make them double this contract in less [than] two years. You can help us all best by keeping out of trouble— it will make a great difference to your important years. Take care of yourself mentally (study when you're fresh), physically (don't pluck your eyebrows), morally (don't get where you have to lie) and I'll give you more scope than Peaches.

Daddy

OCTOBER 8, 1937

Darling Pie:

I'm awfully sorry about that telegram. I got a letter from Bill Warren, saying that it was all around Baltimore that I was making twenty-five hundred a week out here, and it disturbed and upset me. I suppose it was one of Rita Swann's ideas. I don't know why I suspected you—I should have known you would be more discreet and would at least name some believable figure. You see what a reputation you've made with your romantic tales!

As to the missing three days, I really don't blame you for that either. The trouble was that Harold Ober didn't know where you were either. If you had wired him instead of Aunt Rosalind, it would have been all right. However, it gave me only one bad hour, as I really don't fret about you as much as I used to. I did worry about your smoking this summer, but you gave me your word that you wouldn't smoke at Peaches' so that was all right; and I don't care much who you go out with so long as you are in at a decent hour and don't get the practice on your mind. From next summer on, you can find you'll have more privileges, but I don't want them to become habits that will turn and devour you. You have got to devote the best and freshest part of your energies to things that will give you a happy and profitable life. There is no other time but now.

No special news—things have been quiet. Had the questionable honor [of] meeting ———— ————, a shifty-eyed fellow surrounded by huge bodyguards. Norma Shearer invited me to dinner three times but I couldn't go—unfortunately, as I like her. Maybe she will ask me again. Also have seen something of Buff Cobb, Irvin Cobb's daughter, who is an old friend; and Sheilah [1] who, by the way, has broken her engagement to the Marquess Donnegal. (The poor man was about to get on a boat, but it was a sort of foolish marriage in many ways.) Also have been to much tennis and saw Helen Wills come back in company with Von Cramm to defeat Budge and his partner. Took Beatrice Lillie, Charlie MacArthur and Sheilah to the Tennis Club the other night, and Errol Flynn joined us—he seemed very nice though rather silly and fatuous. Don't see why Peaches is so fascinated. Frank Morgan came over and talked to me, telling me that we had a fight in the cloak room at Gloria Swanson's seventeen years ago, but I had no recollection of the incident except that I had a scuffle with somebody. But in those days there [were] so many scraps that this one doesn't stand out in my memory.

I hope you thought over my analysis as to how to deal with the neatness habit, and if for one week you put each thing away individually *from the moment of touching it to the moment of its final disposal*—instead of putting away three things at a time—I think that you would lick it in a month and life would be easier for you in one more way. *Please tell me about this when you write.*

Looking over your letters and answering them in turn—it was nice of Peaches to give a party for you, and I'm glad Stanley is divine-looking; sorry Andrew is repulsive. I'm glad that you went out with that great heart-throb, Bob-

[1] Hollywood columnist Sheilah Graham.

the-Baker. Was Bob Haas nice? Your next letter comes from Exeter. Sorry you can't go to Annapolis—you'll be invited there again. Here I have a postcard and, by God, I'm awfully sore at you about that tutoring. I don't understand how on earth the letter could have been mislaid. I posted it from the airport in Spartanburg that night. So you are still dwelling on the Fisher's Island party in retrospect!

Another letter tells of visiting Mary Earle on Long Island. It sounds fine, but you are right that romantic things really happen in roachy kitchens and back yards. Moonlight is vastly over-estimated. It was all right what you borrowed from Harold. He will put it on my account. So Meredith called from Baltimore! Aren't you afraid of stirring up those old embers? Your disloyalty to Princeton breaks my heart. I sent Andrew football tickets. Your dress sounds fine, Scottie, my bonnie lass.

Lastly, the letter with the Yale postmark—I bet you bought that stationery. It reminds me of something that happened yesterday. On such paper, but with the Princeton seal, I used to write endless letters throughout sophomore and junior years to Ginevra King of Chicago and Westover, who later figured in *This Side of Paradise*. Then I didn't see her for twenty-one years, though I telephoned her in 1933 to entertain your mother at the World's Fair, which she did. Yesterday I get a wire that she is in Santa Barbara and will I come down there immediately. She was the first girl I ever loved and I have faithfully avoided seeing her up to this moment to keep that illusion perfect, because she ended up by throwing me over with the most supreme boredom and indifference. I don't know whether I should go or not. It would be very, very strange. These great beauties are often something else at thirty-eight, but Ginevra had a great deal besides beauty.

I was hoping that they'd get up a "Higher French" course for you. Was nothing done about that? Miss Walker mentioned it in her letter. Your learning German seems to me rather pointless but don't construe this into any tendency to loaf on it. Knowing just a little bit would be a foundation —especially if we go abroad for a few weeks next summer.

I sent the thirteen dollars to Rosalind.

What do you want for your birthday? You might make a suggestion.

I think of you a lot. I was very proud of you all summer and I do think that we had a good time together. Your life seemed gaited with much more moderation and I'm not sorry that you had rather a taste of misfortune during my long sickness, but now we can do more things together— when we can't find anybody better. There—that will take you down! I do adore you and will see you Christmas.

Your loving

[Daddy]

NOVEMBER 4, 1937

Dearest Pie:

I admit I'm a terrible correspondent but I hope it isn't the pot calling the kettle black—i.e., do you write your mother regularly once a week? As I assured you before, it is of the greatest importance, even if Bob-the-Butcher or Bill-the-Baker doesn't get the weekly hook in his gills.

News about the picture: The cast is tentatively settled. Joan Crawford had her teeth in the lead for a while but was convinced that it was a man's picture; and Loretta Young not being available, the decision rests at present on Margaret Sullavan. Certainly she will be much better than Joan Crawford in the role. Tracy and Taylor will be reinforced by Franchot Tone at present writing, and the cameras will presumably roll sometime in December. An old friend, Ted Paramore, has joined me on the picture in fixing up much of the movie construction, at which I am still a semi-amateur, though I won't be that much longer.

Plans about Christmas depend on whether I will be held here for changes through the shooting. I don't think that's probable, and if it weren't my first picture that I'm anxious to get as perfect as can be, I wouldn't let it be possible, because I can always have a vacation on three weeks' notice —but I want to mention it as a very faint chance. However, let us suppose I come East, as I will nine chances out of ten —I will expect to spend the time with you and your mother, perhaps a little in Baltimore, some in Asheville. Maybe I can

31

take your mother to Montgomery, though that is very faint indeed and should not be mentioned to her. Also I want to spend a couple of days in New York and I have no doubt that you will want to be with me then.

Have you any plans of what you'd like to do? Would you like another party in Baltimore? I mean just an afternoon affair like the last. It might become a sort of an institution, a yearly round-up of your Baltimore friends. Write me immediately what you thought you wanted to do —of course you also will go to see your mother sometime during the holidays.

By ill chance the Harvard game tickets for Andrew went astray and were sent me here. I'm sorry. He must have been disappointed—save that he missed the worst drubbing Princeton has had in many years.

My social life is in definite slow motion. I refused a good many parties and am now in the comfortable position of not being invited much any more. I had dinner at Gladys Swarthout's last week with John McCormick and some of the musical crowd. I have taken in some football games with Sheilah Graham, and met the love of my youth, Ginevra King (Mitchell), after an interval of twenty-one years. She is still a charming woman and I'm sorry I didn't see more of her.

How much do the ads cost for your year book? Please let me know.

I have a small apartment now at the Garden of Allah, but have done nothing about the house situation, as there seems no chance of your mother coming out here at the present.

I am anxiously awaiting your first report and will be more inclined to go. . . .[1]

[*Daddy*]

Congratulations on Cheerleader, etc. Can you turn a cartwheel?

---

[1] The rest of the letter is missing, except for the postscript.

Dearest Scottina:

So much has happened out here, and in the East, that a letter can't tell it.

Beginning at the end—*Three Comrades* went into production today and I started on the new Joan Crawford picture—as yet unnamed. I am half sick with work, overwhelmed with it and yet vaguely happier than I've been in months. The last part of a job is always sad and very difficult but I'm proud of the year's output and haven't much to complain of.

Your mother was better than ever I expected and our trip would have been fun except that I was tired. We went to Miami and Palm Beach, flew to Montgomery, all of which sounds very gay and glamorous but wasn't particularly. I flew back to New York intending to take you out with your friends Saturday but I discovered you were on bounds. My zero hour was Monday morning in California so there was nothing to do except fly back on Sunday afternoon. I didn't think you and I could cover much ground with the horses flying around the tan bark and steaming in Rosa Bonheur's steel engraving on the wall.[1]

One time in sophomore year at Princeton, Dean West got up and rolled out the great lines of Horace:

---

[1] Refers to the reception room at Ethel Walker's.

34

"Integer Vitae, scelerisque pueris
Non eget mauris, facule nec arcu—" [2]

—And I knew in my heart that I had missed something by being a poor Latin scholar, like a blessed evening with a lovely girl. It was a great human experience I had rejected through laziness, through having sown no painful seed.

But when anything, Latin or pig latin, was ever put up to me so immediately as your chance of entering Vassar next fall I could always rise to meet that. It is either Vassar or else the University of California here under my eye and the choice is so plain that I have no sympathy for your loafing. We are not even out of debt yet, you are still [a] scholarship student and you might give them a break by making a graceful exit. They practically took you on your passport picture.

Baby, you're going on blind faith, as vain as Kitsy's belief that she wouldn't grow a whisker, when you assume that a small gift for people will get you through the world. It all begins with keeping faith with something that grows and changes as you go on. You have got to make all the right changes at the main corners—the price for losing your way once is years of unhappiness. You have not yet entirely missed a turning, but failing to get somewhere with the Latin will be just that. If you break faith with me I cannot feel the same towards you.

[2] Horace actually wrote:
"Integer vitae, scelerisque purus
Non eget mauris iaculis neque arcu"

35

The Murphys, Nora, etc., asked after you. We will without fail go somewhere at Easter—your mother's going to make a stay in Montgomery with a companion and she'll meet us. Some New York gallery has taken some very expensive pictures of you—do you want any? I like them but my God they cost.

With dearest love always,

Daddy

[*Metro-Goldwyn-Mayer Corporation*]
[*Culver City, California*]

FEBRUARY 22, 1938

Dearest Pie:

I never hear from you any more. Please drop me a line and tell me if all goes well.

I started my new picture which is after all a piece called *Infidelity* and will star Joan Crawford and I don't know who else. I will finish the first draft Easter and will come East to take you somewhere.

Three Comrades is halfway through. I have seen some of the shooting and some of the "rushes" (where they run off what they've shot that day) but you can't tell much from either. To my mind, the producer seriously hurt the script in rewriting it. It may be I am wrong.

People ask after you, but I am the most curious of all. May I be permitted to ask after you? I'd like a line about your health, your work, your morale, success or failure of the play and such affairs. If you will let me know when the play is, I will send you a message of congratulation or flowery tokens if you prefer.

I think of you always, darling, and will try to invent something very nice for Easter.

Just heard from Mrs. Turnbull who said you had three especial qualities—loyalty and ambition were two, the third I'll tell you later. She felt that would protect you from harm. I make no comment. She seemed very fond of you.

Also the Finneys have sent me the work of a musician to do something about, and I am taking the matter in hand.

With dearest love,

Daddy

37

MARCH 11, 1938

Dearest Pie:

I'm glad you got 74. If you had gotten that the first term, we'd have something to start on now. A letter came at the same time from Miss Walker, in which she referred to your "low position in the class." Of course this is not at all what you implied to me when I saw you in January, and I do wish you would be more accurate. To suggest a state of affairs which doesn't exist merely stalls off the final reckoning. The most important thing in your life now is to get good marks at school and pass the examinations for Vassar in June. It is so important that if you don't, I am unable, off-hand, to think of any satisfactory alternative. You will be exactly in the position of a man who has done a bad job and been fired, which will be a nice black mark against you at sixteen. You can't and mustn't let this happen. I am not going to spend Easter lecturing you and this is to forestall any attitude on your part that I am unreasonable not to be appeased by your success in other lines.

On the other hand, I am of course pleased that you did well as Mrs. Bennett (Harold Ober wrote me that your acting stood out). Also, I am glad that the musical comedy you wrote was so successful at school. Why don't you get a volume of Gilbert and Sullivan and read the extraordinary and amazing lyrics of *Iolanthe* and *Patience*. I used to study them like mad when I was writing the Triangle shows at Princeton. (I see, by the way, that a boy named

38

James W. Huntley has been elected to the Cottage Club at Princeton. Did you know him in Baltimore?) I wish I could say as nice things about the poem after Ogden Nash (I dined with him and Bill Leonard night before last). It was a long way after. Ogden Nash's poems are not careless, they all have an extraordinary inner rhythm. They could not possibly be written by someone who in his mind had not calculated the feet and meters to the last iambus or trochee. His method is simply to glide a certain number of feet and come up smack against his rhyming line. Read over a poem of his and you will see what I mean. Your poem has every line in a different meter. One changes from a two-four rhyme to a gallop, to a waltz, and so forth, and the total effect is nil. I know you didn't think much of it but you did send it to me, so I am telling you the truth.

I am glad you have gotten around to liking Dorothy Parker and that you had the good taste to pick out her "Diary of a New York Lady." It is one of her best pieces. As to knowing her, you do know her, but that was in the days when you were a little weary of my literary friends. I knew Elizabeth Firestone's father very well and liked him very much. What are you going to do for the Firestone Tire Hour? Thank God you got a credit for posture. That's really good news. I think you can have the suit that you want for spring. Shall I send you the money or what? Write me immediately.

I think your Pinehurst suggestion is rather good for Easter. Jim Boyd lives at Southern Pines next door; in fact, he owns most of it. We might do a few days there and a few days at Virginia Beach. However, the geographical part of our plans will depend on what the doctor will let your mother do.

Dearest love always.

Daddy

I liked the lyrics you told me last January—very well turned. I suppose they were in the show. Ordered none of those photos—they were so tight-lip one imagined that they concealed gold teeth. I heard there was a flood here but didn't look out the window as I was busy.

Dearest Pie:

Your letter was welcome but I'm sorry you waited to write me until you had nothing pleasant to say—all about hating people, and where you were going to college and how you were about to replace DeMille and Berlin next year. Together with some impertinent cracks about my absurd unreasonableness. I simply conclude that you were in a bad humor because none of it makes much sense.

As to Bryn Mawr, I am entering you at St. Timothy's next year so if you miss at Vassar you will be able to be near Baltimore, which I gather you want. If you thought you were going to spend next year weekending in Baltimore you must have suddenly come to one of those decisions of yours that I am a sucker. I have no such plans for you. Either you accept responsibilities and let me graduate from this unwelcome role of stern father or you stay another year in jail with the children. Your whole liberty turns on the question of your work and nothing else—the kind of talent in demand out here doesn't walk out on a job.

In any case I'm coming East this month and we'll go somewhere and we'll find out your objections to this dog's life you lead and if they're valid we'll change them.

Love,
Daddy

Dearest Pie:

Got your postcard. A couple of days ago got a wire from my old friend, Alice Lee Myers. You remember, the woman who took Honoria and some other girls abroad last summer. She is taking a party this year which will include Fanny, and I think it sounds very good. Traveling is always fun; you always meet young people on the boat and in hotels during the summer, and the trip itself would include a station wagon tour of France, Belgium, Holland, and perhaps a taste of England. I won't mention that it would help your French, because that sounds too much like work, but I will say that if it works out you will be a very lucky girl, for quite possibly these are the last few years in which you will be able to see Europe as it was. Though I may add that if you get caught in a war this summer, I will simply deny knowing you and you will have to get out of it the best way you can; *but please don't start one.*

God, how I'd like to go myself. Everything is work here, just as I expected, and of course I came back without any rest and it was two or three days before I was really able to get going again. I like the work part, but seem to have to do it in big, heartbreaking doses, which is bad for the constitution. Sorry we didn't have as many talks as I had hoped for. You had no special plans for the summer, I gathered, except what general invitations might be available, and I really don't want you out here for the whole summer because there is no Helen Hayes and really nothing much to do that

would interest you except a repetition of last summer—
only less interesting, as I am out of touch with Norma, Joan,
etc. However, if you come for a week in June with
Peaches, I will open up relations again and try to make an
impression on her. I am writing the Finneys today. I
wouldn't talk around school about summer plans until they
are more definite. I will have to bargain with Alice Lee
Myers about the European trip, and for the Hollywood
trip see if Pete will trust his precious into my hands. Your
mother, Obers, etc., are to know nothing yet—the teachers
nothing.

Now the European trip would be due to start either June
22 or July 2nd. I imagine that I could have the dates changed
a little, or rather that, as you are one-fourth of the party, the
time of your examinations would have to be a determining
point in the itinerary. When will they be over? What are the
actual dates? What would you say, if the European trip is decided on, to the idea of leaving school after graduation, coming out here and taking your boards here in Hollywood and
then, if time is short, flying back to New York? I don't mind
your flying now as I did last summer. It is as nearly safe in
June as such things can ever be. *Also, I want a truthful answer as to whether the school would rather you stayed there.*
Please don't make me take this up with Miss Walker. If they
would rather, by a margin of 60-40, that you stayed, I want
to know, and I want to know *now, by airmail.* The marks
were really so very mediocre that, if I was Vassar, I wouldn't
take you unless the school swore that you were a serious
character—and the school is not going to swear you are a
serious character if you let a prep school dance stand even
faintly in the way of your success. Besides, if they don't

43

want you to stay, and the trip abroad works out, I would like to catch a glimpse of you during that time. *I don't want to come East in June if it can possibly be avoided.* After all, you are going to college, so this is not your real graduation. Nobody came to mine, and I don't remember being hurt. Nevertheless, if it were not for all the hazards involved, such as bringing your mother there or else hurting her feelings by not bringing her, and the fact that it may come right at the crucial point of this picture (due to roll in June, but perhaps not starting till the fifteenth), I would love to go and see you standing flowerlike among the other fashionable peonies. Moreover, if it means an overwhelming lot to you, I will try to arrange it, but you can well understand how I dread any repetition of this Easter trip.

I got a vague word from Harold that you were going to "study hard" but I have no word from anybody about whether you took the Latin and how many lessons you took. The report is the same in detail from all your teachers and it is too dispiriting to go into. If you will trust my scheme of making a mental habit of doing the hard thing first, when you are absolutely fresh, and I mean doing the *hardest* thing *first* at the *exact moment that you feel yourself fit for doing anything* in any particular period, morning, afternoon or evening, you will go a long way toward mastering the principle of concentration. It has been so ironic to me in after life to buy books to master subjects in which I took courses at college and which made no impression on me whatsoever. I once flunked a course on the Napoleonic era, and I now have over 300 books in my library on the subject and the other A scholars wouldn't even remember it now. That was because I had made the mental tie-up that work equals something unpleasant, something to be avoided, something to be postponed. These scholars you speak of as being bright are no brighter than you, the great majority not nearly as quick nor, probably, as well endowed with memory and perception, but they have made that tie-up, so that something does not stiffen in their minds at the mention that it is a set task. I am so sure that this is your trouble because you are so much like me and because, after a long time milling over the matter, I have concluded that it was mine. What an idiot I was to be disqualified for play by poor work when men of infinitely inferior capacity got high marks without any great effort.

Write me what you think about the summer plans. The alternative is not sitting around in some attractive suburb with a bunch of Gilman School boys chewing on your ear, pleasant as the prospect might appear. I am afraid you would be somewhat second-hand by autumn, and I prefer you as you are for a little longer.

Dearest love.
*Your Progenitor in
the Direct Line*

Will you kindly touch on *every point* in this letter when you answer it? I am keeping a carbon, hoping you will. This is a time when we ought to be able to communicate— we are unconflicting on 90% of things—all except your lazy belly which my thin gut shrinks from. Please work —work with your best hours.

[*Metro-Goldwyn-Mayer Corporation*]
[*Culver City, California*]

[SPRING, 1938]

Dearest:

I hope Mary Earle won't find the trip too expensive. It *is* if you are not going to Vassar, but if you are I think it will be such a worthwhile thing and I wish to God I could go over with you.

We have reached a censorship barrier in *Infidelity* to our infinite disappointment. It *won't* be Joan's next picture and we are setting it aside awhile till we think of a way of halfwitting halfwit Hays and his Legion of Decency. Pictures needed cleaning up in 1932–33 (remember I didn't like you to see them?) but because they were suggestive and salacious. Of course the moralists now want to apply that to *all* strong themes—so the crop of the last two years is feeble and false, unless it deals with children. Anyhow we're starting a new story and a safe one.

About *adjectives:* all fine prose is based on the verbs carrying the sentences. They make sentences move. Probably the finest technical poem in English is Keats' "Eve of Saint Agnes." A line like "The hare limped trembling through the frozen grass," is so alive that you race through it, scarcely noticing it, yet it has colored the whole poem with its movement—the limping, trembling and freezing is going on before your own eyes. Would you read that poem for me, and report?

I'm having a controversy with the Highland Hospital.

They want to keep your mother there with only six weeks out a year and a few trips with Dr. and Mrs. Carroll. I can't see it—I think she should be out from one-fourth to one-half the time, using the hospital only as a base. If I insist, they threaten to release her altogether to me which would be simply a catastrophe—I can't work and look after her. And she wouldn't obey any companion unless the hospital has authority back of the companion. Mrs. Sayre wants her to come and sit beside what will soon be a deathbed and I can't see that as promising any future (I don't mean Mrs. Sayre is sick but she is almost so). She (your mother) wants to come to your commencement with Newman and Rosalind—O.K. if it can be arranged for a nurse to take her to and from N.Y.

I don't dare at the moment to tell your mother about the Alice Lee Myers trip or the fact that I've taken a shack at the beach here (address Garden of Allah still). She would feel as if we were happy and she was in prison. If only old Carroll was less obstinate—however it should be solved within a few weeks—I may have to go East but God forbid.

A letter from Miss Walker. Never has my intuition so surely informed me of a thing than now—that you are walking on a most delicate line there. No matter how you feel I should play a "straight" role for five weeks, lest they mistake any action for a frivolous attitude. All through life there are such games to play—mine for instance, when I first came here, to keep away from any bars, even though I wasn't tempted to drink. The connection of "bar-drunk" was too easy to establish in people's minds after my past performances. But don't tell your best friend that you are playing a sober role—such things travel fast and far. You will be smart in playing nun for the time being—five weeks will win you many months.

> Dearest love always.
>
> *Daddy*

[*Metro-Goldwyn-Mayer Corporation*]
[*Culver City, California*]

[MAY, 1938]

Dearest Pie:

I'm glad you acted decently in the end about that infirmary affair. We'll consider it closed.

About the college courses, in case you get in—for freshman year at least I want them to be subject to discussion between us—I don't think, for example, that you are ready for philosophy. I made some bad mistakes in choosing my own curriculum on silly careless premises, because courses came at the right time, were rumored easy, etc. I thought I'd [learn to] read Italian to read Dante and didn't get to first base. I should have known from my wretched French that I had no gift for languages. Similarly you went into physics instead of taking more French and you must have been a considerable drag on the rest of the class. So we will discuss your curriculum when we meet. The enclosed is merely to indicate to you that a course in economics might be interesting in these troubled times. I am not insistent about science but at least one line you follow must be useful rather than cultural.

It's been a bad year for you. I hope you'll save the remnants by getting into college and I do wish you wouldn't blame others ever for what happens to you. A famous gunman who was lately electric-shocked from among us said he only shot the policeman because he wasn't let alone. Right up to the chair he thought he was being put upon. You were never anti-social in youth—it is one regard in

49

which this year your reasoning is more like your mother's than mine. Never in her whole life did she have a sense of guilt, even when she put other lives in danger—it was always people and circumstances that oppressed her. I think, though, that you are walking towards some awful sock in the next few months that will have a sobering effect on you and I will be glad when it's over and you are your old modest and charming self again.

Do try to make your mother happy for two days—excuse her enthusiasm. In her youth, she didn't know such schools existed. Tell her you may go abroad if your exams are good.

If you do, and I am very anxious you should, I can't bring you and Peaches out here this June—September would be better. I have no facilities for chaperonage at the moment but if there is cooperation in your heart this summer I will arrange it for next September. I gather Mary Earle's mother wasn't interested in the European trip.

The censors have stopped *Infidelity* as we were about to go into production. I am doing the screenplay of *The Women* for Norma Shearer. My God—what characters! What gossip! Let me remind you never to discuss my affairs with a living soul.

With dearest love,
Daddy

[*Metro-Goldwyn-Mayer Corporation*]
[*Culver City, California*]

JULY 7, 1938

Dearest Scottie:

I don't think I will be writing letters many more years and I wish you would read this letter twice—bitter as it may seem.[1] You will reject it now, but at a later period some of it may come back to you as truth. When I'm talking to you, you think of me as an older person, an "authority," and when I speak of my own youth what I say becomes unreal to you—for the young can't believe in the youth of their fathers. But perhaps this little bit will be understandable if I put it in writing.

When I was your age I lived with a great dream. The dream grew and I learned how to speak of it and make people listen. Then the dream divided one day when I decided to marry your mother after all, even though I knew she was spoiled and meant no good to me. I was sorry immediately I had married her but, being patient in those days, made the best of it and got to love her in another way. You came along and for a long time we made quite a lot of happiness out of our lives. But I was a man divided—she wanted me to work too much for *her* and not enough for my dream. She realized too late that work was dignity, and the only dignity, and tried to atone for it by working herself, but it was too late and she broke and is broken forever.

[1] After graduation, while studying for college boards at Ethel Walker's, Scottie had broken bounds and been asked to leave the school. Fitzgerald's fear that it might prevent her from getting into Vassar occasioned this letter.

It was too late also for me to recoup the damage—I had spent most of my resources, spiritual and material, on her, but I struggled on for five years till my health collapsed, and all I cared about was drink and forgetting.

The mistake I made was in marrying her. We belonged to different worlds—she might have been happy with a kind simple man in a southern garden. She didn't have the strength for the big stage—sometimes she pretended, and pretended beautifully, but she didn't have it. She was soft when she should have been hard, and hard when she should have been yielding. She never knew how to use her energy—she's passed that failing on to you.

For a long time I hated *her* mother for giving her nothing in the line of good habit—nothing but "getting by" and conceit. I never wanted to see again in this world women who were brought up as idlers. And one of my chief desires in life was to keep you from being that kind of person, one who brings ruin to themselves and others. When you began to show disturbing signs at about fourteen, I comforted myself with the idea that you were too precocious socially and a strict school would fix things. But sometimes I think that idlers seem to be a special class for whom nothing can be planned, plead as one will with them—their only contribution to the human family is to warm a seat at the common table.

My reforming days are over, and if you are that way I don't want to change you. But I don't want to be upset by idlers inside my family or out. I want my energies and my earnings for people who talk my language.

I have begun to fear that you don't. You don't realize that what I am doing here is the last tired effort of a man who once did something finer and better. There is not enough energy, or call it money, to carry anyone who is dead weight and I am angry and resentful in my soul when I feel that I am doing this. People like ———— ———— and your mother must be carried because their illness makes them useless. But it is a different story that *you* have spent two years doing no useful work at all, improving neither your body nor your mind, but only writing reams and reams of dreary letters to dreary people, with no possible object except obtaining invitations which you could not accept. Those letters go on, even in your sleep, so that I know your whole trip now is one long waiting for the post. It is like an old gossip who cannot still her tongue.

You have reached the age when one is of interest to an adult only insofar as one seems to have a future. The mind of a little child is fascinating, for it looks on old things with new eyes—but at about twelve this changes. The adolescent offers nothing, can do nothing, say nothing that the adult cannot do better. Living with you in Baltimore (and you have told Harold that I alternated between strictness and neglect, by which I suppose you mean the times I was so inconsiderate as to have T. B., or to retire into myself to write, for I had little social life apart from you) represented a rather too domestic duty forced on me by your mother's illness. But I endured your Top Hats and Telephones until the day you snubbed me at dancing school, less willingly after that. . . .

To sum up: What you have done to please me or make me proud is practically negligible since the time you made yourself a good diver at camp (and now you are softer than you have ever been). In your career as a "wild society girl," vintage of 1925, I'm not interested. I don't want any of it—it would bore me, like dining with the Ritz Brothers. When I do not feel you are "going somewhere," your company tends to depress me for the silly waste and triviality involved. On the other hand, when occasionally I see signs of life and intention in you, there is no company in the world I prefer. For there is no doubt that you have something in your belly, some real gusto for life—a real dream of your own—and my idea was to wed it to something solid before it was too late—as it was too late for your mother to learn anything when she got around to it. Once when you spoke French as a child it was enchanting with your odd bits of knowledge—now your conversation is as commonplace as if you'd spent the last two years in the Corn Hollow High School—what you saw in *Life* and read in *Sexy Romances*.

I shall come East in September to meet your boat—but this letter is a declaration that I am no longer interested in your promissory notes but only in what I see. I love you always but I am only interested by people who think and work as I do and it isn't likely that *I* shall change at my age. Whether you will—or want to—remains to be seen.

Daddy

P.S. If you keep the diary, please don't let it be the dry stuff I could buy in a ten-franc guide book. I'm not interested in dates and places, even the Battle of New Orleans, unless you have some unusual reaction to them. Don't try to be witty in the writing, unless it's natural—just true and real.

P.P.S. Will you please read this letter a second time? I wrote it over twice.

[*Metro-Goldwyn-Mayer Corporation*]
[*Culver City, California*]

[JULY, 1938]

Dearest Pie:

When I wrote down those architectural terms hoping to encourage a "Gothic Quest" I overlooked what was right under my eye. Rotterdam, oddly enough, is the center of modern architecture. J. P. P. Oud, who was invited to give the Kalin lectures at Princeton some years ago, is the greatest living architect in all probability, and his workers' dwellings, designed when he was city architect of Rotterdam, are a model for the world. See them if you come back that way and compare them with New York slums. Also, if this reaches you in Paris, you might find Caffin's easy book on architecture at Brentano's. Please buy it.

Also if you're in Paris when this reaches you, a *pneumatique* might reach Nanny at 23 rue Pascal-Lecointre: I think it would be nice if you took her to lunch. If you do, make her feel happy and important—she did a great deal for you. Give her my love.

I have been trying to get your actual college board ratings. Do you realize now that all that bother about French has saved you one whole year of education? I mean that French was the deciding factor in your skipping a grade. So that if you should marry at 19 you will have had one more year of education than if you had let it slip. I hadn't intended to bring up the college matters definitely in this letter, but, since I've said this, [I] might as well add that you should approach Vassar as if you were going to do

55

the four years. A girl's life is so different from a boy's in America that the odds are incalculable as to whether or not you will take a degree—but who knows? Your mother had a broken engagement on her hands a few days before her nineteenth birthday—what could have been better than to have had something to go on with? It is very exceptional for a grown person to jump straight from one serious love affair into another.

Aside from that—and you know I'd be happy if you didn't marry before twenty at the earliest—I think it would have an effect on your own morale and the feelings of other students toward you if you signed up "for the duration of the war." To half of the girls there, Vassar will be their whole world as Princeton was mine and, though they might enjoy a little butterflying, their resentment against the self-confessed butterfly who is only killing time with them will be very deep in their hearts, and will deepen as the years increase. So I should soft-pedal my social ambitions and ride with the times. After all the president of last year's Vassar senior class just married a Rockefeller and the Clark girl of Boston made her debut as a singer instead of on Beacon Hill. The Bachelors' Cotillion simply doesn't mean what it did twenty years ago—or even ten. I suppose it meant a lot to ——— ——— because she's not likely to have anything any better.

All that is snobbish talk but the part about going in whole-heartedly, and publicly so, is very important and real. I want college to be good—I was pretty discouraged there for a while—I felt myself losing interest, and illness has made me pretty selfish and self-protective. I could see you stranded with a lot of childhood memories—and two thousand trivial letters. I even had a talk with a man who owns a canning factory in San Diego with the idea of giving you the works from the bottom. It would have made you or broken you (i.e., made you run away). But it was pretty drastic medicine and I'm glad I didn't have to resort to it. In an odd way you are an old-fashioned girl, living half in the world of Mrs. Finney and Mrs. Turnbull (you should have seen the latter's face the day the banks closed in '33 and I had the only money on the place—$1800 in gold). Often I have encouraged that because my generation of radicals and breakers-down never found anything to take the place of the old virtues of work and courage and the old graces of courtesy and politeness. But I don't want you to live in an unreal world or to believe that the system that produced Barbara Hutton can survive more than ten years, any more than the French monarchy could survive 1789. Every girl your age in America will have the experience of working for her living. To shut your eyes to that is like living in a dream—to say "I will do valuable and indispensible work" is the part of wisdom and courage.

> With dearest love,
> *Daddy*

P.S. At the *Saturday Evening Post* rate this letter is worth $4000. Since it is for you only and there are so many points, won't you read it twice?

[*Metro-Goldwyn-Mayer Corporation*]
[*Culver City, California*]

SEPTEMBER 19, 1938

Dearest Pie:

Here are a few ideas that I didn't discuss with you and I'm sending this to reach you on your first day.[1]

For heaven's sake don't make yourself conspicuous by rushing around inquiring which are the Farmington Girls, which are the Dobbs Girls, etc. You'll make an enemy of everyone who *isn't*. Thank heaven you're on an equal footing of brains at last—most of the eventual leaders will be high school girls and I'd hate to see you branded among them the first week as a snob—it's not worth a moment's thought. What *is* important is to go to the library and crack your first book—to be among the 5% who will do this and get that much start and freshness.

A chalk line is absolutely specified for you at present because. . . . besides the "cleverness" which you are vaguely supposed to have "inherited," people will be quick to deck you out with my sins. If I hear of you taking a drink before you're twenty, I shall feel entitled to begin my last and greatest non-stop binge, and the world also will have an interest in the matter of your behavior. It would like to be able to say, and would say on the slightest provocation: "There she goes—just like her papa and mama." Need I say that you can take this fact as a curse—or you can make of it a great advantage?

[1] At Vassar.

58

Remember that you're there for four years. It is a residential college and the butterfly will be resented. You should never boast to a soul that you're going to the Bachelors' Cotillion. I can't tell you how important this is. For one hour of vainglory you will create a different attitude about yourself. Nothing is as obnoxious as other people's luck. And while I'm on this: You will notice that there is a strongly organized left-wing movement there. I do not particularly want you to think about politics, but I do *not* want you to set yourself against this movement. I am known as a left-wing sympathizer and would be proud if you were. In any case, I should feel outraged if you identified yourself with Nazism or Red-baiting in any form. Some of those radical girls may not look like much now but in your lifetime they are liable to be high in the councils of the nation.

I think it would be wise to put on somewhat of an act in reference to your attitude to the upper classmen. In every college the class just ahead of you is of great importance. They approach you very critically, size you up and are in a position to help or hinder you in anything you try. I mean the class *just* ahead of you. A sophomore class is usually conceited. They feel that they have been through the mill and have learned something. While this is very doubtful, it is part of wisdom to humor that vanity in them. It would pay dividends many times to treat them with an outward respect which you might not feel and I want you to be able to do such things at will, as it happens that all through life you may be in a position in which you will constantly have to assume a lowly rank in a very strict organization. If anybody had told me my last year at Princeton that I would stand up and take orders from an ex-policeman, I would have laughed. But such was the case because, as an army officer, he was several grades above me in rank and competence— and that is not the last time it has happened.

Here is something you can watch happen during your college course. Always at the beginning of the first term about half a dozen leaders arise. Of these at least two get so intoxicated with themselves that they don't last the first year, two survive as leaders and two are phonies who are found out within a year—and therefore discredited and rated even lower than before, with the resentment people feel for anyone who has fooled them.

Everything you are and do from fifteen to eighteen is what you are and will do through life. Two years are *gone* and half the indicators *already point down*—two years are left and you've got to pursue desperately the ones that point up!

I wish I were going to be with you the first day, and I hope the work has already started.

With dearest love,

[*Daddy*]

[*Metro-Goldwyn-Mayer Corporation*]
[*Culver City, California*]

[FALL, 1938]

Dearest Scottie:

I am intensely busy. On the next two weeks, during which I finish the first part of *Madame Curie,* depends whether or not my contract will be renewed. So naturally I am working like hell—though I wouldn't expect you to understand that—and getting rather bored with explaining the obvious over and over to a wrong-headed daughter.

If you had listened when Peaches read that paper aloud last September this letter and several others would have been unnecessary. You and I have two very different ideas—yours is to be immediately and overwhelmingly attractive to as many boys as you can possibly meet, including Cro-Magnons, natural-born stevedores, future members of the Shriners and plain bums. My idea is that presently, not quite yet, you should be extremely attractive to a very limited amount of boys who will be very much heard of in the nation or who will at least know what it is all about.

The two ideas are *irreconcilable,* completely and utterly inverse, obverse and *contradictory!* You have *never* understood that!

I told you last September that I would give you enough to go to Vassar, live moderately, leave college two or three times during the fall term—a terrific advantage in freedom over your contemporaries in boarding school.

After four weeks I encountered you on a weekend. Here is how it was spent—God help the Monday recitations:

Friday—on the train to Baltimore
            Dance
Saturday—to New York (accidentally) with me
Sunday—to Simsbury to a reunion

The whole expedition must have cost you *much more* than your full week's allowance. I warned you then, as I had warned you in the document Peaches read, that you would have to pay for your Thanksgiving vacation. However, in spite of all other developments—the Navy game, the Dean's information, the smoking, the debut plans—I did not interfere with your allowance until you gave me the absolute insult of neglecting a telegram. Then I blew up and docked you ten dollars—that is exactly what it cost to call you the day of the Yale-Harvard game because I could not believe a word you said.

Save for that ten dollars you have received $13.85 every week. If you doubt this I will send you a record of the cancelled checks.

There is no use telegraphing any more—if you have been under exceptional expenses that I do not know of I will of course help you. But otherwise you must stay within that sum. What do you do it for? You wouldn't even give up smoking—and by now you couldn't if you wanted to. To take Andrew and Peaches—who, I think you will agree, come definitely under the head of well-brought-up children —if either of them said to their fathers: "I'm going to do no favors for you but simply get away with everything I can" —well, in two minutes they'd lose the $25 a month they probably get!

But I have never been strict with you, except on a few

essentials, probably because in spite of everything I had till recently a sense of partnership with you that sprang out of your mother's illness. But you effectively broke that up last summer and I don't quite know where we stand. Controlling you like this is so repugnant to me that most of the time I no longer care whether you get an education or not. But as for making life soft for you after all this opposition— it simply isn't human nature. I'd rather have a new car.

If you want to get presents for your mother, Peaches, Mary Law, Grandmother, etc., why not send me a list and let me handle it here? Beyond which I hope to God you are doing a lot about the Plato—and I love you very much when given a chance.

Daddy

P.S. Do you remember going to a party at Rosemary Warburton's in Philadelphia when you were seven? Her aunt and her father used to come a lot to Ellerslie.

[*Metro-Goldwyn-Mayer Corporation*]
[*Culver City, California*]

NOVEMBER 15, 1938

Dearest Scottie:

I haven't heard from you yet but I'm assuming that your common sense has asserted itself and I'll get a fair answer to my letter. How you could possibly have missed the answer to my first question I don't know, unless you skipped pages 160 to 170 in *Farewell to Arms*. Try again! There's nothing vague in these questions of mine but they require attention. I hope you've sent me the answer to the second question. The third question is based on the book *Ecclesiastes* in the Bible. It is fifteen pages long and since you have it in your room you ought to get through it carefully in four or five days. As far as I am concerned you can skip the wise-cracks in italics on pages 766, 767 and 768. They were written by somebody else and just stuck in there. But read carefully the little introduction on 754 and note also that I do not mean "Ecclesiasticus" which is something entirely different. Remember when you're reading it that it is one of the top pieces of writing in the world. Notice that Ernest Hemingway got a title from the third paragraph. As a matter of fact the thing is full of titles. The paragraph on page 756 sounds like the confession of a movie producer, even to the swimming pools.

Am glad you were reading about Twentieth Century Sophists. You meet them every day. They see their world falling to pieces and know all the answers, and are not going to do anything about it.

Did the quilts come? The Baltimore stuff and also the

one from New York, which, of course, was a duplication as it turned out. Isn't it common courtesy to acknowledge such matters? Also, Harold said he sent you that old *Redbook* story of mine. Did you read it?

Dearest love.

Daddy

P.S. Your failure to send me that slip on the second page gummed up the list of Elizabethan lyrics I'd made, so that there was some repetition in the second list. Your teachers must love you for that splendid casual quality but I don't think you'd hold a job five minutes.

[*Metro-Goldwyn-Mayer Corporation*]
[*Culver City, California*]

NOVEMBER 18, 1938

Dearest Scottie:

I'm certainly glad to catch a glimmer of wisdom in your attitude—even though you unveiled the story of the blow-away pink slip *after* the telegraph company had checked on you. And even though in one page of your letter you had intended to go to Baltimore from Thursday to Saturday, while in another part you hadn't intended to go at all.

I'm sorry about ———'s tea. I've nothing against her except that she rather stuck her neck out about Vassar, which I suppose she is attending for the social prestige involved. She seemed very nice, quite transparent—a type that turned up all too frequently in the Cottage Club at Princeton. I do wish you would find some more interesting friends. To take the curse off your not going to her party I wrote a nice letter to her mother explaining my apparent tyranny in forbidding it. Same to the mother of ——— ———.

In answering my questions you asked some yourself. The one about Baltimore can be answered from *Ecclesiastes*, "There is a time for weeping, a time for laughing," etc. Fourteen was simply not the time for you to run around on evening dates—at least Pete Finney and I thought not in our erroneous ways. The parents of ——— ——— and ——— ——— thought differently. Who is interested in a girl with her bloom worn off at sixteen? The one thing you still re-

66

proach me for is letting you go, against my better judgment, to the dance at St. Andrew's School.

It is now perfectly sensible for you to go with college boys. (I didn't want you to stay in Baltimore this fall because I felt it would shoot you into Vassar with your mind full of gayety or love, which it apparently did, for your first month there was a flat bust. Also, I did not want you to start with a string of football games this fall.) If you are invited to the Yale or Princeton proms this winter or next spring by a reputable boy—and I'm entitled to the name, please—I'd have absolutely no objection to your going.* *The whole damn thing about going to the colleges is to keep it in proportion.* Did you ever hear of a college boy, unless he were an idiot, racing from Smith to Vassar to Wellesley? There are certain small sacrifices for a college education or there wouldn't be any honor in having gone to college.

But the New York thing is as wrong now as the auto date was at fourteen. I will quote you from a letter I wrote Harold Ober: "Those debutante parties in New York are the rendezvous of a gang of professional idlers, parasites, pansies, failures, the silliest type of sophomores, young customers' men from Wall Street and hangers-on—the very riff-raff of social New York who would exploit a child like Scottie with flattery and squeeze her out until she is a limp colorless rag. In one more year she can cope with them. In three more years it will be behind her. This year she is still puppy enough to be dazzled. She will be infinitely better off here with me than mixed up with that sort of people. I'd

* If it doesn't come in an examination week.

rather have an angry little girl on my hands for a few months than a broken neurotic for the rest of my life." But I don't have to tell you this—you probably read the *Life* article on the dim-witted ———— girl and the razz on her in *The New Yorker*.

As to the money. Your full allowance for next Monday, $13.85, will reach you almost as soon as this does. I'm sorry you were inconvenienced at the loss of the $10.00, but it is a trifle compared to the inconvenience you have caused at this end. I will also send an additional $5.00, which will make $18.85 for the Baltimore trip, but that $5.00 will come off the following week's allowance. I want you to stay in Baltimore until Sunday, and I mean specifically in Baltimore, not at Vassar, not at Scarsdale. This money must *absolutely* take care of the Baltimore trip!

Yes, it *is* too bad you have to be checked up on like a girl of ten. I'd hoped you'd be rather different this year. If Peaches hadn't been with you that first day in Hollywood I would have squelched the idea of rooming with a debutante as I had meant to. I let it go because I didn't want to open her visit that way. I'm as sick of this bloody matter as you are. I can just see people pointing at you at New York dances and saying, "That's Scott Fitzgerald's daughter. She likes her champagne young. Why doesn't he do something about it?"

Even if your aims are the most worldly, the road that I am pointing out is the right one. A great social success is a pretty girl who plays her cards as carefully as if she were plain.

> With dearest love,
> *Daddy*

P.S. Please address all future correspondence to my new address, 5221 Amestoy Ave., Encino, Los Angeles, California.

[*Metro-Goldwyn-Mayer Corporation*]
[*Culver City, California*]

NOVEMBER 25, 1938

Dearest Scottie:

I'm concerned about the history test though I know the classroom work *may* have been better. However, at Walkers your tests ran almost equal to your classroom work, usually ahead of it, and finishing early rather indicates that you were out of material, doesn't it? But I feel that if you like that work you can pass it. I never blame failure—there are too many complicated situations in life—but I am absolutely merciless toward lack of effort. That's why I finally lost interest in ——— ———. I'm sending you a book that seems to have helped some people at Princeton. You might glance over it. You must admit that my prophecy has proven true. I said that to get decent grades you would have to study at least as hard as you did between leaving Walkers and taking the board examinations. I don't mean that it will be tough sledding indefinitely but there will have to be a period of tough sledding before you come to Easy Street. Why don't you let it be now? You can still pull out of this hole before Christmas—and put me in a most generous mood.

Knowing your character, here's about the way things will go in the next month. You have four weeks before Christmas and probably you intend to try hard but at the moment you have gotten into some entanglement in Baltimore that you either want to go deeper into or get out of, or put on ice—in any case, that will require two or three days of letter writing and absorption. Then you will do well

70

for three days—until the reply to your letter sets you off again. By now your impetus will be exhausted and you will have a good three-day low—the movies and New York, forget to hand in a theme, or something like that. Two weeks gone. Then, alas, one of those things will happen against which only the wisest will guard—a two-day cold, an unexpected change of Christmas plans, some personal trouble or upset. Then there's only a week left and despite frantic hours you will have another failure on your hands. Don't you see that this is just how it happens? Where's that "common sense" that you boast about?

I begin to wonder about the postal service there. I wrote you some weeks ago that the second question was:

During the retreat from Caporetto, Lieutenant Henry was haunted by one of the poems in the second list, which came into his memory in distorted form. What poem was it?

That should take you only a minute. Also, did you ever get my letter in which I included a letter you wrote me from Walkers last June?

The address given you before is incorrect. The right address is: 5521 Amestoy Ave., Encino, Los Angeles, California.

With dearest love,
Daddy

P.S. $5.00 of the $10.00 advanced you is deducted from this week's check, which please find enclosed.

Dearest Scottie:

A letter from Miss Barber tells me you may very possibly be on probation. I am disappointed but not brokenhearted as it was in the cards from September. In one way you are like me—that when things seemed to be going oh so smoothly they were really slipping from underneath subtly and surely. But on the other hand remember that when you are struggling and fighting and perhaps feeling you are getting nowhere, maybe even despairing—those are the times when you may be making slow, sure progress. I hope December has been one of those times—I hope it is the beginning of an effort that, if the probation *is* imposed, will see it lifted very soon.

I thought the letter from Miss Barber had a somewhat impertinent tone. This is doubtless because you seem to have told her you were *eighteen* which of course would throw an entirely different light on my wishes about New York and make me rather silly. This rather detracted from the sympathy that I first felt for you, which prompted my wire.

Presuming you are hard up I am sending a small advance on your Dec. 19th allowance to keep the wolf from the door.

My plans are all uncertain. Is that Princeton pamphlet any good?

With dearest love,

Daddy

P.S. Your letter came. Touched that you wish I wouldn't worry about the marks and enlightened to know why freshmen are marked hard. "I don't see why you're so furious because I'm not brilliant" is a sentence that touches my heart. I don't know whether it's the thought or the style that impresses me most. Which was your philosophical poem? "Be my little little little, little wife?"

Which reminds me. I sent you the librettos of W. S. Gilbert. What I want you to read is *Patience* which was written as a counterblast of Wilde's asceticism. Did you like the Dowson poem? What notorious modern novel takes its title from a line of it?

About your masterwork—the diary. (Seriously it has some nice writing in it, sharp observation, flashes of wit, etc. I cut pages 1 and 2 from a typed version and sent it to your grandmother.)

The editing I did was slight—names changed (Myers, Murphys, etc.); reference to your mother's not getting well. . . . There is not a word or a line changed—nor even a correction of spelling. Excuse my map—I never did know how you got from Switzerland to Paris.

Who are you going to visit in Baltimore if you go there? I have no time to dig you up stuff about Ernest but his first book *In Our Time* tells a lot about himself. I have not taken a week from your allowance. I wish in your letter now—the last I'll get before vacation—you would tell me *in bulk* just *how much you owe!*

Daddy

Dearest Pie:

I believe you have to deposit this by the third of February. Anyhow as soon as you know you are going on give it to them. I have added the music charges from the catalogue—of course you get no scholastic credit for preliminary music.

I suppose you have finished the essay. If you are still writing it don't forget that the age of marriage is largely a biological question. Girls in India mature at thirteen, in the American tropics at about fifteen or sixteen, and in Scandinavia as late as twenty-one. Most questions in life have an economic basis (at least according to us Marxians), but this is one where biology undermines economics. Hence the Spanish duenna and the French chaperone, because these races realize that while economically it's better to wait, nature in southern lands has quite contrary intentions.

I will take care of the Turnbull matter.

By this time you will have heard from exams. I hope it goes well. You are the first woman on either side of your family to try for a higher education—though many of them have been well-read. If you get to know a little bit you will combine a great deal of latent power in yourself, and be able to live more fully and richly than the majority of pretty girls whose lives in America are lop-sided, backward-looking and wistful.

How about "Cynara," etc.? I feel a slowly mounting exasperation.

My address is simply

          Encino,

          California.

Your letter was a masterpiece of polite evasion.

                        Love,

                         Daddy

Dearest Scottie:

I know you looked first at the check, but it does *not* represent a business transaction. I am too tired at the moment to argue but your figures are wrong. However, I'm having it all checked up by my secretary. I think there is a gift somewhere.

Sorry you got the impression that I'm quitting the movies—they are always there—I'm doing a two-weeks rewrite for Paramount at the moment, after finishing a short story. But I'm convinced that maybe they're not going to make me Czar of the Industry right away, as I thought 10 months ago. It's all right, baby—life has humbled me— Czar or not, we'll survive. I am even willing to compromise for Assistant Czar!

Seriously, I expect to dip in and out of the pictures for the rest of my natural life, but it is not very soul-satisfying because it is a business of telling stories fit for children and this is only interesting up to a point. It is the greatest of all human mediums of communication and it is a pity that the censorship had to come along and do this, but there we are. *Only*—I will never again sign a contract which binds me to tell none other than children's stories for a year and a half!

Anyhow, I'm on the new Madeleine Carroll picture (go to see *Café Society*—it's pretty damn good, I think. This one is the same producer-director-stars combination) and

76

anyhow the movies are a dull life and one hopes one will be able to transcend it.

You've let me down about the reading. I'm sorry you did because I'll have to bargain with you. Read *Moll Flanders*, for any favors asked. I mean this: skip *Tono Bungay* but if you don't care enough about my advice to do some fractional exploring in literature instead of skimming *Life* and *The New Yorker*, I'm going to get into one of those unsympathetic moods—if I'm not sorry for people's efforts there seems to be an icy and inhuman reaction. So please report on *Moll Flanders* immediately . . . meanwhile airmail me another travel folder on Mrs. Draper and her girls. Who is she and they? And who is Moll Flanders?

I hope you enjoy the Princeton prom—please don't be overwhelmingly—but no, I am done with prophecies—make your own mistakes. Let me only say "Please don't be overwhelmingly anything!" and, if you are, don't give my name as the responsible parent! (And by the way never give out any interview to any newspaperman, formal or informal—this is a most definite and most advised plea. My name and you, bearing parts of it, is (are) still news in some quarters—and my current policy, for reasons too numerous to explain, is *silence*. Please do me this courtesy!)

I should like to meet you somewhere early in April—the third or fourth.

Your mother *is* in Florida—it seems to have been delayed.

Of course I'm glad and it warms me all over to know that even ungrammatically "both your French English and history teachers" etc. Though you are pretty completely hatched and I can be little more than your most dependable friend, your actions still have a most decided effect on me and at long range I can only observe you thru the eyes of Vassar. I have been amazed that you do not grasp a certain advantage that is within your hand—as definite as the two-headed Russian eagle—a girl who didn't *have* to have an education because she had the other women's gifts by accident—and who *took one anyhow*. Like Tommy Hitchcock who came back from England in 1919 already a newspaper hero in his escapes from Germany and the greatest polo player in the world—and went up to Harvard in the same year to become *a freshman*—because he had the humility to ask himself "Do I know anything?" That combination is what forever will put him in my pantheon of heroes.

Go thou and do likewise.

Love,
Daddy

Dearest Pie:

Day of rest! After a wild all-night working on *Gone with the Wind* and more to come tomorrow. I read it—I mean really read it—it is a good novel—not very original, in fact leaning heavily on *The Old Wives' Tale*, *Vanity Fair*, and all that has been written on the Civil War. There are no new characters, new technique, new observations—none of the elements that make literature—especially no new examination into human emotions. But on the other hand it is interesting, surprisingly honest, consistent and workmanlike throughout, and I felt no contempt for it but only a certain pity for those who considered it the supreme achievement of the human mind. So much for that—I may be on it two weeks—or two months. I disagreed with everybody about how to do *Madame Curie* and they're trying it another way.

Your cold stirred certain gloomy reflections in me. Like me, you were subject to colds when young, deep chest colds near to pneumonia. I didn't begin to be a heavy smoker until I was a sophomore but it took just one year to send me into tuberculosis and cast a shadow that has been extremely long. I wish there was something that would make you cut it out—the only pay-off is that if you're run down by June to spend a summer in the open air, which is a pity with so much to do and learn. I don't want to bury you in your debut dress.

79

My own plans are uncertain. I am pretty disgusted with pictures after all that censorship trouble and want to break off for a while when I have another good credit (I won't get one on *The Women*)—but *when*, I don't know.

Haven't read *De Monarchia*. Read several pieces by Cornelia Skinner and found them thin and unamusing. Since you've undertaken the *Dorian Gray* I hope you make a success of it but I hope the professor knows what you're doing. She might not consider the rearrangement of some-one else's words a literary composition, which would leave you out on a limb. Are you taking swimming?

Dearest love.

Daddy

P.S. Of course I do not care if you postpone "Cynara," etc., though it's such a detail, and you must be in the library every day. Your college work comes first—but I can't help wondering how, if time is reduced to such minuscules, you would ever have thought of trying out for a play. That of course is entirely out at present—last year should have taught you *that* lesson.

[*5521 Amestoy Avenue*]
Encino, California

MARCH 11, 1939

Dear Scottie:

Thanks for your long letter about your course of subjects.

Generally, I think that your election of French as a major is a wise decision. I imagine that there will be some competition for the Sorbonne but it might be something to aim at. Also, if you want to take one English course I think you have chosen wisely. Once again I concur about the History of Music if it pleases you. But I wish you would thoroughly reconsider the chemistry question. It is an extremely laborious subject—it requires the most meticulous care and accuracy during long laboratory hours. Moreover, unless your mathematics are at your fingertips—and you were never very good at mathematics—you will be continually re-doing experiments because of one small slip, and I just can't see it fitting in with hours of music practice and some regular exercise.

One suggestion is to take *preliminary* physics. I don't know whether, if you have already offered that as an entrance, they would allow it, but they might and it would be a fairly easy running over of it as a very essential and interesting subject. I do not mean that I advise a second-year physics course because that would run into as much mathematics as chemistry. But if, God help us, they insist on a science I should advise you to consider them in the following order: botany, physiology, or child study. Think of

81

the enormous pleasure amounting, almost, to the consolation for the tragedy of life that flowers have been to your mother and your grandmother. Maybe you could be a landscape architect like Lenotre but the personal element is equally important. I felt all my life the absence of hobbies except such, for me as abstract and academic ones, as military tactics and football. Botany is such a definite thing. It has its feet on the ground. And after reading Thoreau I felt how much I have lost by leaving nature out of my life.

I am sorry about the philosophy. I should think that if anything your test questions will deal with the big key figures, and a certain concentration of work upon Plato, Aquinas, and Descartes would pay more dividends than trying to study over entirely the course from the beginning. Please don't give it up as a bad job. Are you sure that you entirely understand the great usages thru the ages of such terms as *nominalists* and *realists?* I want you to keep your interest at least as far as Hegel from whose stem all Marxian thinking flows; certainly you will agree that Marxism does not concern itself with vague sophistries but weds itself to the most practical mechanics of material revolution.

I should suggest that you go to Sea Island with the party and return by yourself, passing at least a full day with your mother in Asheville, and a day, if you like, in Baltimore; that is, I think the Finneys would be a little offended if you did not pay at least a courtesy visit. I shall try my best to be East by the second, and at least cross your path—perhaps in Asheville—but I have let myself be inveigled into another picture and it may possibly run on to the tenth of April; on the other hand it may blow up to-morrow. (It is the new Carroll-MacMurray picture.)

With dearest love,

Daddy

P.S. Can you give me some sort of budget for your trip to Sea Island?

2nd P.S. You are not entirely right about the translations (poetry, of course, cannot be translated, but even there we have exceptions such as *The Rubaiyat*). Constance Garnett's Russian translations are excellent, while Scott-Moncrieff's *Proust* is a masterpiece in itself. And please do not leave good books half-finished, you spoil them for yourself. You shouldn't have started *War and Peace,* which is a man's book and may interest you later. But you should finish both the Defoe and the Samuel Butler. Don't be so lavish as to ruin masterpieces for yourself. There are not enough of them!

[*5521 Amestoy Avenue*]
[*Encino, California*]

[MARCH, 1939]

Dearest Scottie:

I was incredibly happy when I heard that the cloud had lifted. *Don't* let it come down again! I was so happy when it lifted for me at Princeton and let me in for everything I'd wanted that I forgot. And the second time I never did manage to get out of a scholastic mess all the time I was in college. If you don't get *too* happy this spring, don't lose the ground you've gained—it's going to be all right.

Congratulations—I know what it means to you, something you did for and by yourself. A sort of justification. The only excuse for the damper up above is that we have to continue to justify ourselves each week of our lives and it would seem there would be rest sometimes. Did you ever read Christina Rossetti's

"And does the road wind uphill all the way?
  Yes—to the very end—"

I want you to get Peaches a present—rather a useful one. This seems somewhat lavish but this is a world of give and take. I am allowing you twenty-five dollars for it. As it is a lavish gesture it should be a simple present—something she should find practical and useful—on the other angle from a ring-watch. Something that if you hadn't bought it, Pete would have had to buy it. You know her well enough to give her familiar things. Ponder this carefully—if you buy her a "bauble" the idea will defeat its purpose.

Also take your mother something for $15. So I'm sending:

6 days at Sea Island at $13.00 .... $78.00
2 presents $40.00
Railroad fare $100.00
Clothes $50.00
Expenses .... ~~$310.00~~ $50.00
                                                            ———————
                                                            $310.00 (*sic*)

And to cover the airplane I'm making it $350.00. You have no leeway on your incidentals. I know the instinct to delight everybody with a big tip but in the end we too generous people die of heart trouble, trying to make it good, and have rewarded the wrong people, so be a little penurious and calculating with your small change.

I'm just as glad Cottage lost out. They've been dominant for five years—it's time it should be someone else. The only healthy thing about the God-awful system is that no one of the four is triumphant for long. In my time it was Tiger Inn—since then they've all taken turns. Did you run into a man named Ralph Wyer at the prom? He's a Minnesotan and seems to me an altogether admirable fellow. I saw him lose a tooth with great grace at the Dartmouth Winter Carnival in the hockey game.

Your comment on the satirical quality in English fiction is very apt. If you want a counter-irritant read *Bleak House* (Dickens' best book)—or if you want to explore the emotional world—not now, but in a few more years—read

Dostoevski's *Brothers Karamazov*. And you'll see what the novel can do. Glad you like Butler—I liked the place where Ernest's father "turned away to conceal his lack of emotion." My God—what precision of hatred is in those lines. I'd like to be able to destroy my few detestations— ————, for example—with such marksmanship as that.

Again thanks for wiring me. I must love you a lot for you have quite a power to lift me up and cast me down.

Jove,

(Sometimes known as Jupiter or "Papa Angelicus")

[5521 Amestoy Avenue]
[Encino, California]

APRIL 5, 1939

Dearest:

Thanks for your letter.

When you get time give me a sort of budget of what you did with the money I sent you. I mean, estimate roughly what became of it. Also, did you take any planes to and from Sea Island or Asheville? As I wrote you, most of those eastern lines are safe after the first of February. In spite of the storm you ran into on the way back East last fall, I think it's rather old-fashioned not to get used to airplane travel and use it as a convenience.

You made a great impression on your mother. How different from a year ago at Virginia Beach when you seemed as far apart as the poles, during those dreary tennis games and golf lessons! Of course, the fact that she is so much better accounts for a good deal of it, but I believe that was the time you had first discovered love, in the person of ——— ———, and were in a sort of drugged coma until you could get back to Baltimore.

Spring was always an awful time for me about work. I always felt that in the long boredom of winter there was nothing else to do but study. But I lost the feeling in the long, dreamy spring days and managed to be in scholastic hot water by June. I can't tell you what to do about it— all my suggestions seem to be very remote and academic. But if I were with you and we could talk again like we used to, I might lift you out of your trouble about concentration. It really isn't so hard, even with dreamy people like you and me—it's just that we feel so damned secure at times as long as there's enough in the bank to buy the next meal, and enough moral stuff in reserve to take us through the next ordeal. Our danger is imagining that we have re-sources—material and moral—which we haven't got. One of the reasons I find myself so consistently in valleys of depression is that every few years I seem to be climbing uphill to recover from some bankruptcy. Do you know what bankruptcy exactly means? It means drawing on re-sources which one does not possess. I thought I was so strong that I never would be ill and suddenly I was ill for three years, and faced with a long, slow uphill climb. Wiser people seem to manage to pile up a reserve—so that if on a night you had set aside to study for a philosophy test you learned that your best friend was in trouble and needed your help, you could skip that night and find you had a reserve of one or two days' preparation to draw on. But I think that, like me, you will be something of a fool in that regard all your life, so I am wasting my words.

Query: Are you taking up the swimming during the spring term? I hope tremendously you will, but I suppose that's been decided already. If not, what are you doing for spring athletics?

Query No. 2: Is there any way—and don't kid me—in which you can take driving lessons? Also, if you get time —and this is not important—give me a slight picture of what the life is at Sea Island. Also, when you get time, write your mother, because I've been putting off a visit to her and may possibly have to be here three weeks longer on this damned picture and she probably feels that I'm never coming.

Dearest love always.

Daddy

P.S. Got a nice thank-you letter from Frances Turnbull for the check I sent her.

Dearest:

I am sending you four weeks' allowance and hope you can make it go. Found your very sweet letter when I got back. *Please* pay up your debts in full. You know if things get really out of hand you can always call on me, but I am in for a little siege of illness and I will have to count pennies for a few months until this time is over, so don't splurge on any new big spring wardrobe.

Plans for June all depend on factors that I am absolutely unable to regulate now. Literally, I do not know what we are liable to do. In spite of the fact that I have this house and may possibly bring your mother out here for a month or so (now this must absolutely not be mentioned in any letter to her because everything is ready by the hospital and I haven't yet divulged any plans to Dr. Carroll) I still don't see you out here. You see, it would inevitably force us into that old relationship which was unsuccessful five years ago in Baltimore of my being more or less in the unpleasant position of a spy on your private affairs.

I am turning over several possibilities in my mind. One of them is would you like to go to Russia with a group of girls on an economically organized tour? I am sure such things must be going on at Vassar and you need only make inquiries about it and give me the data. I mean something for three or four weeks. I agree that I don't want you to go back to France this summer. But it might just be an experience to go to Russia on some non-deluxe affair. Form your own opinion about how the experiment might work out. I have several more strings to my bow, but I am not telling you all of them at once. But Hollywood—why?

What do you want to do out here? I can no more see you as a reader in a studio wading through bad novels and worse magazine stories all summer and being so dog-tired at the end of the day that you would probably be ready for anything, even these empty-headed California boys. The question of getting you a test has occurred to me too, but I have got at least three or four reasons against it. First, I believe you ought to wait another year—second, I want you to have one more year at Vassar and then make your debut in Baltimore. Suppose you were good? Then it would completely upset the applecart which we have elaborately set up back East. And what else can you do out here? Do you want to come out and be my secretary? *Let us laugh quietly and mirthlessly with a Boris Karloff ring.* As for some of the ideas you had before, it skips my mind whether we discussed them, but I remember one of them was whether you should go to summer stock in one of those New England towns. Honey, I may as well hand you over to the white slavers and make a thorough job of it. For girls like you, it is nothing but a complete playtime job and strong competition between the girls to see who gets the honor of being seduced by the leading man.

Doubtless all sorts of ideas have occurred to you and, if so, why not list them and send them to me—maybe we will find out of them one that fits both our ideas.

I think I have answered almost everything in your letter and I have another idea about the driving which I am going

to leave for another month because it seems to me almost
dangerous for a girl your age not to know how to drive.

Dearest love.

Daddy

[*5521 Amestoy Avenue*]
[*Encino, California*]

[JULY, 1939] [1]

My plan would be to start you out here the last day of the month—that is ten days from the time of writing this letter. The only thing that would prevent this would be some unexpected turn of illness. This is unlikely, but possible. I don't know how this trip is going to work out and feel a certain trepidation. I am of course not drinking and haven't been for a long time, but any illness is liable to have a certain toxic effect on the system and you may find me depressing, over-nervous about small things, and dogmatic —all these qualities more intensified than you have previously experienced them in me. Beyond this I am working very hard and the last thing I want at the end of day is a problem while, as it is natural at your age, what you want at the end of the day is excitement. I tell you all this because lately we had planned so many meetings with anticipation and they turned out to be flops. Perhaps forewarned will be forearmed.

If the experiment proves upsetting I will have no further choice than to pack you off East somewhere again, but there are several friends here whom you could visit for a time if we failed to make a satisfactory household. So the trip will be worthwhile. Also I am more of a solitary than I have ever been but I don't think that will worry you

[1] The first part of this letter is missing.

because you had your dosages of motion picture stars on two other trips. To describe how humorless I feel about life at this point you have simply to read the Tarkington story called "Sinful Dadda Little" in the *Post* issue of July 22 (still current, I believe) and remember that I read it without a particle of amusement but with a complete disgust at "Dadda" for not drowning the two debutantes at the end.

Probably I am underestimating you, as everyone seems to be pleased with your good manners and your "attitude" (I know you hate that word) this summer—notably Mrs. Owens and your mother. But you left a most unpleasant impression behind last autumn with many people, and I would much rather not see you at all than see you without loving you. Your home is Vassar. Anything else to be supplied at present is a mockery of a home. It is too bad it should be this way but the only thing is to treat it as a visit and for us both to remember the rules of common courtesy toward each other. I take my sleeping pills regularly between eleven and twelve so we won't have any of those midnight wrangles that disfigured your June and September visits. Can't the party wait till you get here to discuss? Beneath all this, you understand, I have so much to talk to *you* about. (Incidentally, your memory has played you false about the philosophy. If the taking of it was a mistake it was mine not yours. I chose it one day when we were sitting on my bed with the catalogue at the beach a year ago. And I had some correspondence with Vassar trying to get you into the course at all. The history and French are as much a mystery to me as you say they are to you.)

Please give your mother this enclosed letter when you are alone with her as I don't want it to go through the sanitarium. (Changed. Am writing her [Zelda] separately. Enclosed is for yours and her expenses at boarding house.)

With dearest love,
Daddy

P.S. I am pretty definitely breaking with Ober but he doesn't know it yet.

I am certainly glad that you're up and around and sorry
that your selection of post-Flaubertan realism depressed you.
I certainly wouldn't begin Henry James with *The Portrait
of a Lady* which is in his "late second manner" and full of
mannerisms. Why don't you read *Roderick Hudson* or
Daisy Miller first? *Lord Jim* is a great book—the first third
at least and the conception, though it got lost a little bit in
the law-courts of Calcutta or wherever it was. I wonder if
you know why it is good? *Sister Carrie*, almost the first piece
of American realism, is damn good and is as easy reading as
a *True Confession*.

I wish I could say the same about a recent article in
Mademoiselle. I grant you the grace of having been merely
a dupe as I warned you you would be—for I cannot believe
that you would announce that you pursued your education
yourself while I went around to the speakeasies. There's
nothing to do about it now, but in future please call yourself
by any name that doesn't sound like mine in your writings.
You must have wanted fifty dollars awfully bad to let them
print such a trite and perverted version of your youth, unless
you mean that it was the Fred Astaire pictures that taught
you that gallant stance upon "your own two feet." This
isn't in the nature of quarreling but you certainly owe me
an explanation because I see no earmarks of the "dutiful
daughter" about any of it.

[1] The first part of this letter is missing.

By the time you get this it will be the eleventh. Your plan was to leave for California the fourteenth—your mother's has varied between a trip to Virginia Beach and a quiet time at Saluda. Both of you have something on me because I can't quite decide what *is* best. I am waiting to hear from Montgomery about the exact state of your grandmother's health and also to make up my mind how much work I can undertake in the studios and under what conditions—a matter which depends on X rays, the willingness of the studio to let me work at home, and other such factors.

I want to have you out here for part of the summer. I have a nice cottage in the country, but very *far* out in the country, and utterly inaccessible if one doesn't drive well. Whether a piano here would be practical or not I don't know (remember how I felt about radio) but all that might be arranged if the personal equation were not doubtful (a situation for which for the moment I take full blame). Since I stopped picture work three months ago, I have been through not only a T.B. flare-up but also a nervous breakdown of such severity that for a time it threatened to paralyze both arms—or to quote the doctor: "The good Lord tapped you on the shoulder." While I am running no fever above 99, I don't know what this return to picture work is going to do and when and if my health blows up you know what a poor family man I am. It seems best—and I am merely feeling my way as I write this letter—for you to spend at least another week in the East and you might as well spend it in or near Asheville, especially as it gives your mother such a great pleasure. A long pilgrimage with her would almost certainly require a nurse and run into expense as all trips that your mother and I make have a way of doing.

However, if things seem more stabilized out here to-ward the end of this month I may change my mind and bring you out here and let your mother go to Montgomery. For the moment, there is nothing for you to do but wait and get along as well as possible with your music and writing and what money I can send you. I have a bill from Dr. Hamman for $25.00. Either he was very dilatory or you didn't go to see him till the end of your visit in Baltimore for his diagnosis arrived the day of the operation and it was money thrown away. He seemed to agree, however, that four times out of five you would have had eventual trouble with the appendix.

I have sent for your marks. If you get them, airmail them to me. If they average around "B" I should think you've done well in pulling yourself out of a very difficult hole.

You can read as much or as little of this letter to your mother as you want. I don't mean it to be disagreeable, but I was naturally surprised when instead of carrying out your announced intention of writing about the difference between northern and southern girls you chose to ride on my shoulder and beat me on the head with a wooden spoon.

Your bank statements came through. I noticed there were half a dozen slips marked "insufficient funds." Marshall Neilan, once an ace director out here, went to jail for that little failing last week. These are days when if you haven't got it you better do without. Sorry about Meredith too—I always liked him. The Ober mix-up accounts for his recent coolness. I'm sorry—we got along pretty well for twenty

years. ——— isn't smug or even stuffy—he's a nice adolescent who married a smooth-faced ——— person.

Love,
Daddy

P.S. Sent Peaches a nice present. Was going to do the same
for the ——— girl but John gave me a "subtle" talk about
some dim-witted brother who was reformed by a year in a
drink sanitarium, and almost got his bottom kicked on 33rd
Street.

5521 *Amestoy Avenue*
Encino, California

OCTOBER 31, 1939

Scottina:

(Do you know that isn't a nickname I invented but one that Gerald Murphy concocted on the Riviera years ago?) Look! I have begun to write something that is maybe great, and I'm going to be absorbed in it four or six months. It may not *make* us a cent but it will pay expenses and it is the first labor of love I've undertaken since the first part of *Infidelity*. (Do you remember that half-finished script the censor stopped that I showed you in Norfolk two years ago last Easter? You read it in the cabin of one of those Baltimore-Norfolk liners.)

Anyhow I am alive again—getting by that October did something—with all its strains and necessities and humiliations and struggles. I don't drink. I am not a great man, but sometimes I think the impersonal and objective quality of my talent and the sacrifices of it, in pieces, to preserve its essential value has some sort of epic grandeur. Anyhow after hours I nurse myself with delusions of that sort.

And I think when you read this book, which will encompass the time when you knew me as an adult, you will understand how intensively I knew your world—not *extensively* because I was so ill and unable to get about. If I live long enough I'll hear your side of things but I think your own instincts about your limitations as an artist are possibly best: you might experiment back and forth among the arts and find your niche as I found mine—but I do not believe that so far you are a "natural."

So what? These are such valuable years. Let me watch over the development a little longer. What are the courses you are taking? Please list them. Please cater to me. Please do not ask me to rise to heights of nervous energy—in which I can usually discern the name of the dye on your instructor's hair at long distance or reconstruct the murder of March, 1938, from a rag and a bone and a hank of hair. But give me some outlines.

a. What do Obers say about me? So sad?
b. What is this about my telling Mrs. Owens you were a heel?
c. What play are you in?
d. What proms and games? Let me at least renew my youth!
e. As a papa—not the mad child of a mad genius— what do you do? and how?
f. What furniture? Do you still want etchings?
g. What did Rosalind write?
h. Do you want a test here?
i. Did you ever think of calling on the Murphys to make *them* happy—not to deprecate ———?

I'm glad you read Malraux. Did you get the driver's license? Is Mary Earle nice? I got an instant impression in Connecticut of a brave, lovely, impish person. . . .

With dearest love,
Daddy

5521 *Amestoy Avenue*
Encino, California

NOVEMBER 4, 1939

Dearest Scottie:

Sorry my letter crossed yours—I mean the letter where I said you were not "a natural." If you brought or helped to bring off the show there, I am more than pleased. Without sentimentality, I think it would be nice to give Vassar something back of what it has given to you.

The only important questions in my letter were about your relations in Baltimore; I want to know about the formality of the presentations because, naturally, I will have to send appropriate gifts, etc.

Answer me that question, and also I would like to know how big a part you played in the show.

I have been trying to think of a name that is better for you than "Paint and Powder Club." What do you think of calling it the "Song and Story?" Not so good—or is it?

I am sorry I wrote you that letter. Again let me repeat that if you start any kind of a career following the footsteps of Cole Porter and Rodgers and Hart, it might be an excellent try. Sometimes I wish I had gone along with that gang, but I guess I am too much a moralist at heart and really want to preach at people in some acceptable form rather than to entertain them.

Will send you a small check herewith.

Dearest love.

Daddy

Dearest Scottie:

Communication having apparently ceased from your end, I conclude that you are in love. Remember—there's an awful disease that overtakes popular girls at 19 or 20 called emotional bankruptcy. Hope you are not preparing the way for it. Also I have a bill from a doctor which includes an X ray. Have you had a cough? Please give me a little information, no matter how skimpy.

You have earned some money for me this week because I sold "Babylon Revisited," in which you are a character, to the pictures (the sum received wasn't worthy of the magnificent story—neither of you nor of me—however, I am accepting it).

Dearest love always.

Daddy

FEBRUARY 19, 1940

Dearest Scottie:

Delighted that you're working on a play. In answer to a query in one of your past letters I do like Thomas Mann —in fact I had put his *Death in Venice* on that list I gave you last summer. Have sent your treasurer his check.

I was very interested to hear about Kilduff. Let me know what becomes of Andrew in the club elections. Things are still very vague here.

With dearest love,

F. S. Fitz

Have paid Peck & Peck & Peck & Peck & Peck.

MARCH 15, 1940

Dearest Scottie:

No word from you for some time but I suppose a letter will cross this. I think it was you who misunderstood my meaning about the Comrades. The important thing is this: they had best be treated not as people holding a certain set of liberal or conservative opinions but rather as you might treat a set of intensely fanatical Roman Catholics among whom you might find yourself. It is not that you should not disagree with them—the important thing is that you should not argue with them. The point is that Communism has become an intensely dogmatic and almost mystical religion and whatever you say they have ways of twisting it into shapes which put you in some lower category of mankind ("Fascist," "Liberal," "Trotskyist") and disparage you both intellectually and personally in the process. They are amazingly well-organized. The pith of my advice is: think what you want, the less said the better.

I am sorry about the physiology. There is no answer except the advice that I used to give you constantly in your less receptive days: that sometimes you can lick an especially hard problem by facing it always the very first thing in the morning with the very freshest part of your mind. This has so often worked with me that I have an uncanny faith in it.

No particular news. The Sayres are of course delighted that your mother is coming out. Your mother said something in her letter about spending vacations with you. As you know, I will not have this, except in the most limited fashion. I think the pull of an afflicted person upon a normal one is at all times downward, depressing and eventually somewhat paralyzing, and it should best be left to those who have chosen such duties as a life work. So if there are any inquiries from that source about your summer plans I think it would be wise to answer them in the most general terms, even hinting that you had work mapped out in the North.

With dearest love,
Daddy

P.S. When does your Easter vacation begin? This is very important. Don't forget to tell me about the fate of Turnbull and other Baltimoreans—and about the play.

MARCH 18, 1940

Dear Scottie:

Thanks for your very full letter. Of course I am terribly curious to hear about the show and how big a success it was —for I don't doubt that it was a success, and I think your idea to found a sort of Triangle was most ingenious and energetic and exactly the sort of thing that gives me great pride in you. The satiric theatre is perhaps a better method of expression for you than journalism and perhaps it is just as well that you did not get on the *Miscellany* board. Naturally I would give anything to see the play but will await your description of it when I see you.

Am enclosing $75.00, which I hope will cover your vacation. Negotiations on the screenplay of "Babylon" are still in course. If they should go through and you should be in Baltimore a week from now I would like you to go to Asheville and spend a night with your mother. As things are now I can't afford it but we will see.

Thanks for the news about the Princeton boys. Colonial is a good club, older than Cap and Gown, in fact. At one time people used to refer to the "Big Five," but in my day Colonial got an unfortunate drinking reputation. Now I believe it specializes in boys out of the social register who don't quite make the grade in the big time. I hope Andrew is happy there, though I don't doubt that he is a little disappointed. If I were you I should not discuss the matter with him at all. I still think it is a lousy cruel system.

We'll discuss the summer later. It so much depends on how much money I have. I think that doubtless some movie job could be found for you out here. Competent people with a little pull have no trouble finding places in the small income brackets. It is when your price is $1000 and up a week that it is another story. However I'm not exactly sure it's the best thing.

I will attend to those New York bills when the first money comes in. I wish you would write me immediately *where* you will be during vacation. I mean the approximately exact dates so that I can reach you by wire in case it is feasible for you to go to North Carolina.

Dearest love.

Daddy

P.S. I wish very much you would call on the Murphys during your spring vacation. If there is any way in which you could help Honoria [1]—to a date, for instance—I think it would be mutually very advantageous. Of course, it shouldn't look as if the suggestion came from me. I know it is difficult to pick up an old thread after an interval but it would please me immensely if you could at least pay a call there.

[1] The Murphys' daughter.

MARCH 27, 1940

Dear Scottie:

I am going to work on "Babylon" at a lousy salary—a week from Monday. Anyhow it's something.

A letter from Baltimore disturbed me this morning—what have you done to your hair? Three different people have seen fit to correspond with me about it. Can't you tone down the effect a little? You heightened it so gradually that I don't think you realize yourself now just what it looks like. Nobody minds if a woman over thirty wants to touch hers up but why imitate a type that is passé even in pictures? It was a cute trick when you had one blond strand that looked as if the sun might have hit it, but going completely overboard defeats any aesthetic purpose.

Best luck for the spring term. I know it's always the hardest and I have that almost uncanny fear for you at the moment that comes sometimes. Perhaps it's the touch of overconfidence and self-justification in your letters (i.e., the Daisy Chain) that I haven't seen for over a year. *Please* give yourself a margin for hard luck.

Love,
Daddy

P.S. I can *understand* the overconfidence—God haven't I had it? But it's hard as hell to recognize it in oneself—especially when time's so short and there's so *much* we want to do.

[5521 Amestoy Avenue]
[Encino, California]

APRIL 11, 1940

Dearest Pie:

Thanks for your letter. I'm writing this on a Sunday night, *sans Francoise* [1] and I hope you can read it. I go to cinema work tomorrow on a sort of half-pay, half-"spec" (speculation) business on my own story "Babylon Revisited." Which is to say Columbia advances me living money while I work and if it goes over in installments with the producer, the company, the releasing people, I get an increasing sum. At bottom we eat—at the top the deal is very promising.

Why I'm writing tonight is because I foresee three months of intensive toil. (I feel like a criminal who has been in a hideout, been caught, and has to go back to the Big House. I've been visited by my crooked doctor and my moll and Frances the Fence has protected me. Now the Big House—oh Jees them guards!)

To put you in a good humor for the ensuing gratuitous though friendly advice, let me say I got a letter from *Andrew* today, out of two years' silence, in which he "judges you objectively" as a very fine girl. I was pleased naturally and wish they hadn't counteracted the work I did on him by sending him to a school with a professional Holy-Joe for headmaster. His letter would make you very conceited—shall I send it? You seem to be a big shot down there.

[1] Frances Kroll, Fitzgerald's secretary for the past year.

The advice consists of this— ———— ————'s name bobs up in so many of your letters that I assume he plays a big part in your life, no matter how seldom you see him. I've naturally formed a picture of him—vaguely I associate it with my relation with Marie Hersey at about your time of life. I think she told herself that I was hers for the *special* effort. But they had become matter-of-fact to me—lesser girls would have rivalled them for new excitement and any-one who summed them up, or seemed to [me] like your mother, would simply have washed them out of my mind.

Supposing ———— to be self-absorbed, charming, suc-cessful, and full of the same psychology I had—how defi-nitely handicapped you might be in counting on him! By the very fact of old familiarity, old experience in common, it would be difficult, for men, if they're alive, are con-tinually looking for the new. I mean that he might, so to speak, meet the Queen of Abyssinia in his travels. And how can you rival her?

I'm not driving at the obvious answer of having many strings to your bow. I suppose you have. But haven't you taken ———— as the only *type?* Women are capable of loving three or four types of masculine excellence like the women in *Candida* and *Strange Interlude.* You ought to have, for example: as a cold intellectual, someone who's made the *Harvard Law Review*—you can find him with a little effort. He'll probably be taken already but it can be done. The point is that you have not exhausted any other type at its best except ————; you have only examined the second-rate unproved man of other species (————, ————, etc.). You should know the young predatory business type, hard as hell. He will lick you maybe but you should know him.

A lead at Princeton would be one of the Ivy boys—not Harvey, but he might be a wedge—a boy inheriting a big business.

All the above is probably very obvious so forget it. Are any of the enclosed friends of yours?

Dearest love.

Daddy

P.S. Have paid the Wallace Co. $35.00 and Altmans $40.00 on account. The printed enclosure reminded me that if you have occasion to drive, I forgot to tell you that in the rain *don't depress the clutch*—use the brake *only*. And on hills —go down in the gear in which you'd have come up. I am moving in town to be near my work, so will you address me care of my new agent, Phil Berg, 9484 Wilshire Boulevard, Beverly Hills, or General Delivery, Encino, as they will forward it? Will write you as soon as I have a permanent address.

[5521 Amestoy Avenue]
[Encino, California]

APRIL 12, 1940

Dearest Scottie:

I'm sorry about the tone of the telegram I sent you this morning, but it represents a most terrific worry. You are doing exactly what I did at Princeton. I wore myself out on a musical comedy there for which I wrote book and lyrics, organized and mostly directed while the president played football. Result: I slipped way back in my work, got T.B., lost a year in college—and, irony of ironies, because of scholastic slip I wasn't allowed to take the presidency of the Triangle.

From your letter I guess that you are doing exactly the same thing and it just makes my stomach fall out to think of it. Amateur work is fun but the price for it is just simply tremendous. In the end you get "Thank you" and that's all. You give three performances which everybody promptly forgets and somebody has a breakdown—that somebody being the enthusiast.

Please, please, please delegate every bit of the work you can and keep your scholastic head above water. To see a mistake repeated twice in two generations would be just too much to bear. This is the most completely experienced advice I've ever given you. What about that science and the philosophy? You've got to find hours to do them even if you have to find a secret room where you can go and study.

Dearest love always.

Daddy

113

[*5521 Amestoy Avenue*]
[*Encino, California*]

APRIL 27, 1940

Dearest Scottina:

I am of course delighted about the play. Now that it is over I can admit that I thought it was quite a conception from the beginning and quite an achievement—I just had a moment when I was afraid that you were wearing yourself out over it. Musical comedy is fun—I suppose more "fun" than anything else a literary person can put their talents to and it always has an air of glamor around it.

I was particularly interested in your line about "feeling that you had lost your favorite child." God, haven't I felt that so many times. Often I think writing is a sheer paring away of oneself leaving always something thinner, barer, more meager. However, that's not anything to worry about in your case for another twenty years.

I am glad you are going to Princeton with whom you are going. I feel you have now somehow jumped a class. Boys like Kilduff and Lanahan are on a guess more "full of direction" than most of the happy-go-luckies in Cap and Gown. I don't mean more "ambition," which is a sort of general attribute of youth and is five parts hope to five parts good will, but I mean some calculated path stemming from a talent or money or a careful directive or all of these things, to find your way through the bourgeois maze—if you feel it is worth finding. Remember this, though, among those on both sides of the fence there are a lot of slow developers, people of quality and distinction whom you should not

114

overlook. Particularly you will find them among those of difficult exteriors like Eleanor Turnbull or of a great pervading shyness or personal ugliness, etc. I certainly had to dig under a bushel of spoiled blackberries to find ———— ———— at Princeton and often the same in later life. Needless to say I've made bad mistakes—one of them was ———— ————.

I was going to speak to you about the summer plans —without anything special to contribute. Could you let me know more specifically about the New England idea? Who would you be with? What girls? I know you could make up a lot of names but please tell me pretty specifically what would be the housekeeping set-up? I think I could manage to back something like that. I rather hate to think of you out here unless you were going right out for money by displaying your person in celluloid. It is a half-tropical and listless atmosphere.

I am working on this "Babylon Revisited" picture at a rotten salary but it is rather fun and may amount to something. Your mother seems happy to be home. I don't expect the trouble to begin for at least two months.

With dearest love,
Daddy

MAY 4, 1940

Dearest Scottina:

Glad you got a break in the New York papers. Bet you were thrilled. Notice you got the [?] picture into the background to show you were a glamor girl at heart. No kidding, it was a good job. All I hope is you don't flunk out. You are always welcome in California though. We are even opening our arms to Chamberlain in case the British oust him. We need him for Governor because we are afraid the Asiatics are going to land from Chinese parasols. Never mind—Santa Barbara will be our Narvik and we'll defend it to our last producer. And remember, even England still has Noel Coward.

I actually have a formulating plan for part of your summer—if it pleases you—and I think I'll have the money to make it good. I'm working hard, guiding by the fever which now hovers quietly around the 99.2 level, which is fairly harmless. Tell Frances Kilpatrick that though I never met her father he is still one of my heroes in spite of the fact that he robbed Princeton of a football championship single-handed—he was probably the greatest end who ever played football. In the future please send me clippings even though you do crack at me in the course of your interviews. I'd rather get them than have you send me accounts of what literary sour bellies write about me in their books. I've been criticized by experts including myself.

I think I've about finished a swell flicker piece. Did you read me in the current *Esquire* about Orson Welles? Is it funny? Tell me. You haven't answered a question for six letters. Better do so or I'll dock five dollars next week to show you I'm the same old meany.

Honestly, Pie-crust, I'm tickled about the play. I hope to God your health is good.

Love,
Daddy

P.S. Enclosed 50¢ in stamps to buy the *Esquire* with the Orson Welles piece.

[5521 *Amestoy Avenue*]
[*Encino, California*]

MAY 7, 1940

Dearest Scottie:

We write to each other without ever answering the other's questions. For once I'll answer one of yours. You ask me whether I thought that in the Arts it was greater to originate a new form or to perfect it. The best answer is the one that Picasso made rather bitterly to Gertrude Stein:

"You do something first and then somebody else comes along and does it pretty."

In the opinion of any real artist the inventor, which is to say Giotto or Leonardo, is infinitely superior to the finished Tintoretto, and the original D. H. Lawrence is infinitely greater than the Steinbecks.

Last thought about your review. You will be interviewed again and once more I ask you please do not discuss your mother or myself even faintly with them. You once made the astounding statement that you were immediately going to write our biographies. I'll always agree with myself that I would never write anything about my own father and mother till they had been at least ten years dead, and since I am forty-three and may still have a lot to say for myself I think you'd be somewhat premature. I realize that you are now fully mature and would realize the unwisdom of talking about family affairs consciously—but sometimes these newspaper people twist things out of you.

My movie progresses and I think it's going to be damn

good. If your summer plans mature in any way keep me in the know. I send you a bonus of five dollars, not for any reason but simply because a letter without a check will probably seem to you half-filled. If you have no need for it just add it to your bank account.

Dearest love.

Mad Fitz (once the Scourge of
the San Fernando)
(Daddy)

Dearest Scottina:

Unfortunately the stub of the money order was just *the one* of many that Frances happened to have misplaced (she has all the others). I've threatened her and great tears are oozing out of her eyes as she takes this dictation. However, even if it hadn't been lost it would have been impossible to do much about a signed money order, especially from this end. I hope you went into the Vassar post office branches and identified yourself and put the clerks on watch. So don't let it worry you. I lose ten dollars which is all in a day's work and you lose the five which I was giving you as a bonus. A little later I'm going to ask you to send me a summary of your bills—not that I'll be able to pay them all immediately but I'd like to know how you stand at the term's end. Please try to address me *c/o* Phil Berg Agency, Wilshire Boulevard, Beverly Hills. That isn't so hard to remember.

You confused me rather about your summer plans. If you were rooming with Mary Earle does that mean Cape Cod or does it mean at Vassar under Miss Hallie Flannigan? If it means Cape Cod I know some particularly interesting people up there—not at all the kind that are called "old friends" whom you automatically are prejudiced against but some people who might open many rather camouflaged gates to you—some that your contemporaries don't know about. I'm signing up for an apartment in the middle of

Hollywood where there is a spare room for any wandering daughter, though if you come out here it should be for a reason as it is a dreary town for anyone with nothing to do.

I'm glad you didn't start going to Princeton at sixteen or you'd be pretty jaded by this time. Yale is a good year ahead of Princeton in sophistication, though, it should be good for another year. Though I loved Princeton I often felt that it was a by-water, that its snobby institutions were easy to beat and to despise and unless I was a natural steeplechaser or a society groom I'd have to find my own private intellectual and emotional life. Given that premise it is a lovely quiet place, gentle and dignified, and it will let you alone. Of course, it is at its absolute worst in the Jane Hall atmosphere you described. Sometime go down with a boy on one of those weekends when there's almost nothing to do.

You've had a good year, haven't you—the fruition of a great deal that went before. I'd love to see you and just talk a blue streak with you for about two days about plans if we could afford it financially which we can't. But who can tell, maybe by late June or July we can. Please arrange to see your mother at the earliest possible time because I think those are going to be restless days for her. You don't neces-sarily have to meet her in Montgomery. Perhaps you could meet somewhere else halfway. If there could be some ar-rangement where she wouldn't be entirely left out and you wouldn't be away with some boy at all hours.

Dearest love.

Daddy

MAY 18, 1940

Dearest Scottie:

No word from you this week. I do want to hear all about your plans. Can you see your mother before you go to Baltimore? You say you want eight days. If you're planning a sylvan idyll or doing anything rash like throwing away your honeymoon in advance—well, I can't do anything about it except advise you that women from Aphrodite to Kitty Foyle have tried it impulsively and found that they threw away their lifetime with their honeymoon. I know it's none of my business any more and I hope to God that I'm speaking out of turn. But you seemed so particularly fervent about it.

Isn't it funny how different things are after only six months. For example, wasn't your suggestion to the *Miscellany* board people about changing their paper rather like suggesting to the local church that it would be more fun if it were a burlesque house? And didn't they take it about the same way, only more drily? I mean, you seem much wiser month by month and I don't think you would have gone about it quite that way now. You would have made the paper first, posing as being in complete agreement and *then* throwing your bomb. Did you see in *Time* that the editor of the *Yale News* and nine other boys threw Bones this spring and aren't you glad now that Vassar hasn't a formal social system? .... [1]

[1] The rest of the letter is missing.

Dearest Scottie:

Thank you for your letter. Planning from week to week, I am not quite sure yet about anything, but go ahead about the summer school, make reservations and so forth. I think it can be managed all right. I went to San Francisco with some friends for one day, and found it much too long to see that singularly second-rate and uninspired Fair—though they had some good Cranachs and El Grecos in the art exhibition.

Vassar's only fault to the outer world is the "Vassar manner"—which of course is founded on the sense of intellectual intensity that you mention. I found it particularly annoying in ———— ————'s daughter in Tryon some years ago. She told me all about American literature in the first half hour I met her—I believe she had been editor-in-chief of the *Miscellany* the year before. Of course it does not usually show itself like that, but, like the Harvard manner of 1900 which gave Harvard a country-wide unpopularity, makes itself known in a series of smug silences. Southern manners *are* better—especially the rather punctilious deference to older people. The chances are that some toothless old codger who doesn't open his mouth may turn out to be the greatest authority in the world on some recondite subject, and you feel rather a fool when you have judged him and settled his hash with the glossy learning of a year or so. So be

123

careful of it, especially this summer when you will meet many idiots, some in hysterical panic about the war and others too dumb to know what is going on.

You credit me with a gift of prophecy I don't have. I *did* feel the war was coming in '39 and said so to a lot of people, but it was calculated by the time when Germany would have several new replacement classes to make up for the decreased birth-rate from 1915 to 1918. We all knew the German army wasn't beaten and Woodrow Wilson didn't want it to be beaten, not appreciating the utter helpless decadence of the English—something that has been apparent to even English intellectuals for twenty years. The intellectuals, those few who ever dabbled in military affairs, knew that the war was lost at Munich and that the Germans would tear the Allies to pieces, in Europe at least. And the American rich will try to betray America in exactly the same way as the British conservatives. A pogrom could be organized overnight against all the "subversive elements" (whose power is tremendously overestimated at the moment) but the rich will have to have the pants scared off them before they stop skulking in their tents and begin to get their boys safe jobs in the quarter-master department.

The Comrades out here are in a gloomy spot; ——— ——— goes around groaning how "the Revolution will have to come the hard way," in other words the party line is to let National Socialism (Nazism) conquer us and then somehow milk Marxism out of Hitler's sterile teats! Stalin has pulled another boner just as he did in Finland. He had no intention of letting Hitler go this far.

With the situation changing as fast as it does now, it is

difficult for Liberals to have a policy. The war may lead to anything from utter chaos to a non-Comintern American Revolution, but the world that I knew and that you have had eighteen years of will never exist again in our time. On the other hand I do not think it possible for the Germans to win the South American war against us. The native Yankee is still the most savage and intelligent fighter in the world. He plays the toughest, hardest games with a cooler head and it is simply unthinkable that an oppressed stock could be whooped up in one decade to conquer him. Still I think many of your friends will probably draw their last breaths in Paraguay or the forests of the Chaco. Did you see that Lehman has called for anti-aircraft defense for New York? What a cowardly panic! Next we will have Louis B. Mayer calling for anti-aircraft guns to defend Metro.

This letter has turned into gossip, and I have much to do. I finished the picture and am doing a short story. Had intended to rest for a week, but there wasn't a chance. Dear, I have had a very depressed letter from your mother and another from your grandmother—the second told me in cautious language that your mother had had a "toxic attack." I know what this means, only I expected her to hold out at least two months. She seems to be recovered from that, but her own letter shows a great deal of despair, and your grandmother's has a defeatism that I have never seen before. I don't know what is going to happen, but as this may be the last time you have a chance to see your mother in a sane period, *I want you to find ten days to spend with her this June.* This may bust hell out of your plans, but remember that for ten months you have lived for yourself and you owe this to me. I don't care when you go, except it is to be before summer school opens, and not just three or four days.

The *Harper's* business is all right for me if you can fit it in with everything else. Will you tell me what you are going to take at summer school? I think I wrote you that I thought your next year's Vassar course is fine, except for the Greek Civilization and Literature, which seems to me a profound waste of time. Your other three courses are so completely cultural that I wish that the fourth could be as practical a one as Vassar offers—I wish they had business school—or else a supplementary French course or another language. Greek Civilization and Literature is something you cannot learn in nine months, and it seems to me a rather dilettantish way of wasting time.

I expect to hear in a day or so whether I am going back to work on my picture story—I told you once it was an old *Saturday Evening Post* story called "Babylon Revisited" that I wrote in 1931. You were one of the principal characters.

With dearest love,

Daddy

JUNE 12, 1940

Dearest Scottina:

Thanks for your nice full letter—it made me happy, and I don't doubt your sincerity about work. I think now you will always be a worker, and I'm glad. Your mother's utterly endless mulling and brooding over insolubles paved the way to her ruin. She had no education—not from lack of opportunity because she could have learned with me—but from some inner stubbornness. She was a great original in her way, with perhaps a more intense flame at its highest than I ever had, but she tried and is still trying to solve all ethical and moral problems on her own, without benefit of the thousands dead. Also she had nothing "kinetic," which, in physics, means internal driving force—she had to be led or driven. That was the tired element that all Judge Sayre's children inherited. And the old mother is still, at times, a ball of fire!

I could agree with you as opposed to Dean Thompson if you were getting "B's." Then I would say: As you're not going to be a teacher or a professional scholar, don't try for "A's"—don't take the things in which you can get "A," for you can learn them yourself. Try something hard and new, and try it hard, and take what marks you get. But you have no such margin of respectability, and this borderline business is a fret to you. Doubt and worry—you are as crippled by them as I am by my inability to handle money or my self-indulgences of the past. It is your Achilles' heel

—and no Achilles' heel ever toughened by itself. It just gets more and more vulnerable. What little I've accomplished has been by the most laborious and uphill work, and I wish now I'd *never* relaxed or looked back—but said at the end of *The Great Gatsby:* "I've found my line—from now on this comes first. This is my immediate duty—without this I am nothing." . . . .

Please wire me what days you have chosen to go South so I can make financial arrangements.

Can't you tell some story down there that it's urgently necessary to go to summer school because you've been on the edge of flunking out? Otherwise they'll wonder why the money couldn't be spent for a seaside vacation for you all. I'm living in the smallest apartment here that will permit me not to *look poor,* which I can't afford to do in Hollywood. If the picture goes through, I will give your mother a trip in August. At the moment I am keeping her on a slender allowance, as for ten years she has absorbed the major portion of the family income.

I *did* listen to the radio all through my trip. Jesus! What a battle!

Please at least go in to see Gerald Murphy at Mark Cross for five minutes in passing thru N.Y. this summer!

Send me the details about Harvard Summer School. Can I pay in installments?

Even as a construction man, Pinero was inferior to both Shaw and Ibsen. What purpose is served in teaching that second-rate Noel Coward at Vassar?

The *New Yorker* story might hamper you if you attach too much importance to it. The play *was* an accomplishment

—I admit it with pride and pleasure. I'd like to see the story. *Can't you send me a copy?*

Reading over your letter, you don't sound like an introvert at all. You sound a little flushed and overconfident, but I'm not worried.

With dearest love,
Daddy

P.S. You want to go to summer school. I will have to do extra work for that, and I'll do it gladly. But I want you to spend ten days with your mother first. And *please* give me a *full* complete report on your mother's condition. Your request for $15.00 just came as I was putting this in an envelope. To get it to you (Frances is away) cost me my morning. You must not ask me to wire you money—it is much harder to get than last summer. I owe *thousands*. I couldn't have had this trip except that the Rogers were going and invited me. Sorry to close the letter this way but you must count your pennies.

Dearest Scottie:

Here is your round trip fare to Montgomery. I'm sorry it can't be more but, while my picture *is* going to be done, the producer is going to *first* do one that has been made for the brave ——— ——— who will defend his country in Hollywood (though summoned back by the British government). This affects the patriotic and unselfish Scott Fitzgerald to the extent that I receive no more money from that source until the company gets around to it; so will return to my old standby *Esquire*.

Meanwhile I have another plan which may yield a bonanza but will take a week to develop, so there's nothing to do for a week except try to cheer up your mother and derive what consolation you can in explaining the Spenglerian hypotheses to Miss ——— and her fellow feebs of the Confederacy. Maybe you can write something down there. It is a grotesquely pictorial country as I found out long ago, and as Mr. Faulkner has since abundantly demonstrated.

Anyhow they need you. I will dig you out in time for the summer school.

Love,
Daddy

P.S. As I said, I am trying to give you $30.00 a week this summer, and when there is a lot of traveling to be done will increase this somewhat. For instance, I gave you $20.00 extra to get out of Vassar and there is $10.00 extra in this check which makes $30.00 and which will cover a good deal of transportation to date (including the round trip fare to Montgomery). Will send the next check there.

Dearest Zelda and Scottie:

I wish I were with you this afternoon. At the moment I am sitting rather dismally contemplating the loss of a three-year-old Ford and a thirty-three-year-old tooth. The Ford (heavily mortgaged) I shall probably get back according to the police because it is just a childish prank of the California boys to steal them and then abandon them. But the tooth I had grown to love.

In recompense I found in *Collier's* a story by myself. I started it just before I broke my shoulder in 1936 and wrote it in intervals over the next couple of years. It seemed terrible to me. That I will ever be able to recover the art of the popular short story is doubtful. At present I'm doing a masterpiece for *Esquire* and waiting to see if my producer can sell the "Babylon Revisited" screenplay to Shirley Temple. If this happens, everything will look very much brighter.

Scottie, I got the marks and was naturally pleased you were off probation at last. It brought back memories of phoning you from Los Angeles to see if you were at the Harvard game, of the dean's gloomy picture a year ago last October, of years of distress about your work with threats and prayers and urgings and rewards and apologies and promises and then suddenly the first change about a year ago when you found that Vassar didn't care whether you studied or not—or whether you stayed in or not. It is a story

of hair-breadth escapes, and extraordinary devices going
back to the French schedule that we had at La Paix. All
sorts of people have been drawn into it. Hours, days and
weeks have been consumed. Stories, scripts, trips have been
put aside—all to achieve what might have been prevented if
I had carried out my first plan—never to let you go near an
American school, or else I should have let you become a
doll. I couldn't leave you hanging—

The police have just called up telling me they've recovered my car. The thief ran out of gas and abandoned it
in the middle of Hollywood Boulevard. The poor lad was
evidently afraid to call anybody to help him push it to the
curb. I hope next time he gets a nice, big, producer's car
with plenty of gas in it and a loaded revolver in each side
pocket and he can embark on a career of crime in earnest. I
don't like to see any education left hanging in the air.

Enclosed find four checks, two of which (including one
of yours, Scottie) should go to Mrs. Sayre for provisions,
etc. By Monday I should be able to make some plans for
you, Scottie. Meanwhile you will have written whether you
would like to go to Harvard alone which I do not think
should frighten you. You have those two Vassar credits to
make up if you are going to get an A.B. degree and I
presume this would do it.

From the larger attitude one doesn't know from day
to day what the situation will be. We may be at war one
week after the extinction of the British, an event which at
present writing seems scarcely a fortnight away. It will
probably mean our almost immediate embroilment both in
Northern Canada and Brazil and at least a partial conscrip-
tion. Scottie, you've been as lucky as anybody could be in

your generation to have had a two months' look at Europe just before the end and to have gotten in two years of college in times of peace before such matters are drowned in the roar of the Stuka bombers. And you have seen the men's colleges as they may not be again in our time, with the games and proms. Maybe I'm speaking too quickly—if the British hold out two months until we can get aid to them— but it looks to me as if our task will be to survive.

Even so I would rather you didn't get tied up in any war work except of a temporary nature for the present. I want you to finish your education. If you have any plan for this summer that displaces summer school and is actually constructive please tell me immediately but I know you want to do something.

My thoughts are not so black as this letter sounds— for instance I'm now going to break off and hear the Louis and Godoy fight which will prove Black Supremacy or Red Indian Supremacy or South American Inca Supremacy or something. I hope you are swimming a lot. I can't exercise even a little any more; I'm best off in my room. But I love to think of you two diving from great heights and being very trim and graceful in the water.

With dearest love to all,

{ Scott
{ Daddy

Dearest Scottie:

There's no time to write you a long letter or to answer yours. Only about the summer school:

It seems important that either you take what will tend to give you a definite credit at Vassar or else have a practical tinge. You mentioned economics—I don't know what kind of economics are taught there but the whole science is in such process of dissolution with new laws being built up overnight that if you take it be sure and get a smart man— I mean a brilliant man and preferably a young one. I know a month is a very short time or there are several suggestions I might make. Not being on the spot I can't advise you but only say that I hope it won't be any form of intellectual needlework.

As soon as you get a minute, write me your circumstances there.

With dearest love,
Daddy

Dearest Scottie:

Jib is not spelt gyb. And beyond everything you have sinned in omission by not giving me the correct financial data and I expect an apology. Literally I had $12.00 in the bank for most of that week and it was very unpleasant.

Max Perkins writes me that Jane and three classmates are coming here and want to see something of the movies. I don't know who to introduce them to except Shirley Temple with whom I spent the day yesterday. (Her mother was there so it was all right.) She really is a sweet little girl and reminds me of you at 11½ when you hadn't succumbed to the wiles of Fred Astaire, lovey dovey and the radio crooners. But I told her mother it wouldn't be long now. I don't know whether she's going to do my picture or not.

Haven't you got a carbon of the *New Yorker* article? I've heard that John Mason Brown is a great favorite as a lecturer and I think it's very modern to be taking dramatic criticism though it reminds me vaguely of the school for Roxy ushers. It seems a trifle detached from drama itself. I suppose the thing's to get *really* removed from the subject, and the final removal would be a school for teaching critics of teachers of dramatic criticism.

Isn't the world a lousy place?—I've just finished a copy of *Life* and I'm dashing around to a Boris Karloff movie to cheer up. It is an inspirational thing called *The Corpse in the Breakfast Food*.

Once I thought that Lake Forest was the most glamorous place in the world. Maybe it was.

With dearest love,
Daddy

JULY 18, 1940

Dearest Scottie:

This summer has shown among other things that your education to date is entirely theoretical. I have no general quarrel with this and I believe it is as it should be in preparing for any sort of literary work. However the odds are against your having the type of talent that matures very quickly—most of my contemporaries did not get started at twenty-two, but usually at about twenty-seven to thirty or even later, filling in the interval with anything from journalism [or] teaching [to] sailing a tramp-schooner and going to wars. The talent that matures early is usually of the poetic [type], which mine was in large part. The prose talent depends on other factors—assimilation of material and careful selection of it, or more bluntly: having something to say and an interesting, highly developed way of saying it.

Looking at the problem from short range only, you see how difficult it was to get a job this summer. So let's see what Vassar's got. The first thing that occurs to me is Spanish, which is simply bound to be of enormous value in the next ten years. Every junior-high-school child in California gets a taste of it and could beat you out of a job in South America if we expand that way. It is enough like French so that you have few alphabetical troubles, is pronounced as written, and has a fairly interesting literature of its own. I mean it's not like studying Bulgarian or Chippewa or some strange dialect in which no one had ever had anything to say. Don't you think this would be a much wiser move than the Greek and Latin culture?—the which shocks me that Vassar has such a namby-pamby "course."

I wonder if you've read anything this summer—I mean any one good book like *The Brothers Karamazov* or *Ten Days That Shook the World* or Renan's *Life of Christ*. You never speak of your reading except the excerpts you do in college, the little short bits that they must perforce give you. I know you have read a few of the books I gave you last summer—then I have heard nothing from you on the subject. Have you ever, for example, read *Pere Goriot* or *Crime and Punishment* or even *The Doll's House* or *St. Matthew* or *Sons and Lovers?* A good style simply doesn't form unless you absorb half a dozen top-flight authors every year. Or rather it *forms* but, instead of being a subconscious amalgam of all that you have admired, it is simply a reflection of the last writer you have read, a watered-down journalese.

Don't be too hard on Princeton. Harvard produced John Reed but they also produced Richard Whitney who I like to believe would have been spotted as a punk at Princeton. The Honor System sometimes has a salutary effect on light-fingered gentry.

With dearest love,
Daddy

[*1403 North Laurel Avenue*]
[*Hollywood, California*]

JULY 29, 1940 [1]

I am still on the Temple picture and will continue on if a very avaricious gent named ———— will loosen up. If he doesn't, I will rest for a week, and can stand it as my cough has become a public nuisance.

I wonder who was the ex-Westover woman you met. I wasn't responsible for Ginevra getting fired but that's the way of a legend—it was some Yale boys.

This job has given me part of the money for your tuition and it's come so hard that I hate to see you spend it on a course like "English Prose since 1800." Anybody that can't read modern English prose by themselves is subnormal —and you know it. The chief fault in your style is its lack of distinction—something which is inclined to grow with the years. You had distinction once—there's some in your diary—and the only way to increase it is to cultivate *your own garden.* And the only thing that will help you is poetry which is the most concentrated form of style.

Example: You read *Melanctha* which is practically poetry and sold a *New Yorker* story—you read ordinary novels and sink back to a Kitty-Foyle-diary level of average performance. The only sensible course for you at this moment is the one on English Poetry—Blake to Keats (English 241). I don't care how clever the other professor is, one can't raise a discussion of modern prose to anything above tea-table level. I'll tell you everything she knows about it in

[1] The first part of this letter is missing.

140

three hours and guarantee that what *each* of us tells you will be largely wrong, for it will be almost entirely conditioned by our responses to the subject matter. It is a course for clubwomen who want to continue on from *Rebecca* and Scarlett O'Hara.

Strange Interlude is good. It was good the first time, when Shaw wrote it and called it *Candida*. On the other hand, you don't pass an hour of your present life that isn't directly influenced by the devastating blast of light and air that came with Ibsen's *Doll's House*. Nora wasn't the only one who walked out of the Doll's House—all the women in Gene O'Neill walked out too. Only they wore fancier clothes.

Well, the old master wearies—the above is really good advice, Pie, in a line where I know my stuff. Unless you can break down your prose a little it'll stay on the ill-paid journalistic level. And you can do better.

Love,
Daddy

P.S. Understand me, I think the poetry courses you took in school (and I read the booklets) were utterly sissified drool. But a real grasp of Blake, Keats, etc., will bring you something you haven't dreamed of. And it should come now.

Dear Scottie:

Jane Perkins passed through and happened to mention that she had taken that Blake-to-Keats course—I became less enthusiastic about it because she said they studied Amy Lowell's biography which is a saccharine job compared to Colvin's. However, in the catalogue I see a course called #217 in verse writing. It says, "limited to twelve members —permission required" and it gives only one point. Is that at all practical? I imagine there would be some latitude in the poets that you would read. There is also that Shakespeare course (165) and one in French Poetry (240), one point. Some of the history and philosophical courses look good to me but—oh, hell I can't advise you from this distance. I'm just sorry you can't read some poetry.

It isn't something easy to get started on by yourself. You need, at the beginning, some enthusiast who also knows his way around—John Peale Bishop performed that office for me at Princeton. I had always dabbled in "verse" but he made me see, in the course of a couple of months, the difference between poetry and non-poetry. After that one of my first discoveries was that some of the professors who were teaching really hated it and didn't know what it was about. I got in a series of endless scraps with them so that finally I dropped English altogether.

Poetry is either something that lives like fire inside you —like music to the musician or Marxism to the Communist

—or else it is nothing, an empty, formalized bore around which pedants can endlessly drone their notes and explanations. "The Grecian Urn" is unbearably beautiful with every syllable as inevitable as the notes in Beethoven's Ninth Symphony or it's just something you don't understand. It is what it is because an extraordinary genius paused at that point in history and touched it. I suppose I've read it a hundred times. About the tenth time I began to know what it was about, and caught the chime in it and the exquisite inner mechanics. Likewise with "The Nightingale" which I can never read through without tears in my eyes; likewise the "Pot of Basil" with its great stanzas about the two brothers, "Why were they proud, etc."; and "The Eve of St. Agnes," which has the richest, most sensuous imagery in English, not excepting Shakespeare. And finally his three or four great sonnets, "Bright Star" and the others.

Knowing those things very young and granted an ear, one could scarcely ever afterwards be unable to distinguish between gold and dross in what one read. In themselves those eight poems are a scale of workmanship for anybody who wants to know truly about words, their most utter value for evocation, persuasion or charm. For awhile after you quit Keats all other poetry seems to be only whistling or humming.

You still have that French typewriter in storage, haven't you? Would it be any good? We rent one here and it costs only $5.00 for three months. You threaten to send *me* money! If you have any extra, pay your bills in Poughkeepsie. My suggestion is that after you visit Miss Doyle, you go to Lake Forest and from there go South to Montgomery. I'm afraid the latter seems to be necessary. Your mother most particularly asked to see you again and the only alternative would be to send her North to see you, which means sending *two* people. I know it will be dull going into that hot little town early in September—but you are helping me. Even invalids like your mother have to have mileposts—things to look forward to and back upon. It gives her more pride there in Montgomery if you come to see her, something to talk about. Only think how empty her life is and you will see the importance of your going there. Will you figure out what the fare to Chicago will be?

You wrote me such a full letter that I haven't answered it all even now. When we get some breathing space here I'll have Frances figure how much you cost this year.

Dearest love.

Daddy

P.S. Be careful about showing my letters—I mean to your mother for instance. I write you very freely.

AUGUST 12, 1940

Dearest Scottina:

I'm sorry I didn't mention the story—I'm *glad* you sold it but I thought you were disappointed that you didn't sell it to a big magazine. I suggested disposing of it to some Vassar paper—do you remember?—just for the sake of getting into print and getting some opinions on it. I'm glad you got some money too. I thought of it as a sort of practice composition but I felt a personal interest in it, not having forgotten the nights we worked over it.

I saw your picture in *Harper's Bazaar* and I'm glad you got the job. Working among the poor has differing effects on people. If you're poor yourself you get their psychology and it's broadening—for example, when a boy of the bourgeoise ships before the mast on a tramp-schooner where he has to endure the same privations as the seaman, undoubtedly he achieves something of their point of view forever. On the contrary, a Bennington girl spending a month in slum work and passing weekends at her father's mansion in Long Island gets nothing at all except a smug feeling that she is Lady Bountiful.

I was interested in your Cape Cod conquest. Theoretically a girl has her widest range of choice from about 19 years, 6 months, to 20 years, 6 months—or so I figure. The 18-year-old girl *seems* to have, because she has a stag line after her, but actually she has probably collected less *eligibles* than a slightly older girl. Of course, with the war there may be a tendency among your generation to rush into things. There were lots of quick marriages in 1918. Most of the men came back—but there are a few "class boys" from my class at Princeton who never saw their fathers.

Enclosed is a Vassar paper about the Spanish. Do remember that, with a new language, the first week *when you learn the structure* is the important time. I believe that if you study Spanish hard for a fortnight, even at the expense of everything else, you can coast along on it pretty easily the rest of the year, but if you don't get the verb forms right and the declensions it will start getting mountainously hard inside of a month and will become your cross. I discovered this in Italian at Princeton—neglecting it and then trying to catch up too late. Result: I flunked it hopelessly and never did learn it. However, I'm glad you're taking a chance.

With dearest love, always,

Daddy

Dearest Scottina:

I can imagine the dinner party. I remember taking Zelda to the young ———'s when we were first married and it was a pretty frozen dish, though in general the places we went to even from the beginning were many flights up from the average business man's *menage*. Business is a dull game and they pay a big price in human values for their money. They are "all right when you get to know them." I liked some of the young Princeton men in business but I couldn't stand the Yale and Harvard equivalents because we didn't even have the common ground of the past. The women are empty twirps mostly, easy to seduce and not good for much else. I am not talking about natural society women like Mary Harriman Rumsey and Sara Murphy and some others who made their lives into pageants, almost like actresses.

However, you seem wise enough to see that there is something in ———'s angle. College gives you a head start, especially a girl, and people are not in any hurry to live and think your way. It's all a question of proportion: if you married an army officer you would live half a lifetime of kow-towing to your inferiors until your husband made his way to the top. If, as the chances are, you marry a business man—because for the present business absorbs most of the energetic and attractive boys—you will have to play your cards properly in the business hierarchy. That was why I have always hoped that life would throw you among law-yers or men who were going into politics or big-time jour-nalism. They lead rather larger lives.

Advertising is a racket, like the movies and the broker-age business. You cannot be honest without admitting that its constructive contribution to humanity is exactly minus zero. It is simply a means of making dubious promises to a credulous public. (But if you showed this letter to ———— it would be the end of everything in short order, for a man must have his pride and the *more* he realizes such a situation the *less* he can afford to admit it.) If I had been promoted when I was an advertising man, given enough money to marry your mother in 1920, my life might have been alto-gether different. I'm not sure though. People often struggle through to what they are in spite of any detours—and pos-sibly I might have been a writer sooner or later anyhow.

You haven't given me much idea of ————. Would he object to your working—outside the house I mean? Ex-cluding personal charm, which I assume, and the more con-ventional virtues which go with success in business, is he his own man? Has he any force of character? Or imagina-tion and generosity? Does he read books? Has he any leaning toward the arts and sciences or anything beyond creature comfort and duck-shooting? In short, has he the possibilities of growth that would make a lifetime with him seem attrac-tive? These things don't appear later—they are either there latently or they will never be there at all.

I'm *not* asking these questions to be answered, but only to suggest again that if he is a fairly standardized article, you will find plenty of them during the next year—more than you ever met before—and eighteen is still young to commit yourself.

I think I have a job with 20th Century, which may be a long one. I will know Monday. I'm deducing that you received some money from *Harper's* because you give me no idea of the state of your finances. Anyhow I'm enclosing $15.00. When you get this letter please night letter me how much it will cost to get to Montgomery. I would suggest that you go as follows: take the evening boat from New York to Norfolk, spending a day or night with Ceci, and then go from there to Montgomery or to Atlanta as you like. Certainly before you see all those walking neuroses you can spend a day with the Taylors who have always liked you so much. The trip to Norfolk by boat from New York is really damn nice. You come into Chesapeake Bay and Hampton Roads from a different angle—almost like an ocean voyage and the ship is larger and nicer than the little ferry boats from Baltimore. Also the price is reasonable—less than railroad.

Dear, even in joking I don't like you to use the expression "nervous breakdown" about any emotional struggle you may have to pass through in the next couple of years. Is your generation so soft that they talk of going to pieces if life doesn't always present itself in terms of beautiful, easy decisions? Most girls of your generation and your mother's and your grandmother's have had to decide difficult things at your age and it is silly to think that it is any strain peculiar to yourself. The young men are just as bad—some of them talk about having nervous breakdowns if they are conscripted. But *you* didn't cut your milk teeth on an aspirin tablet and I hate that raspberry sundae diction. Face what you've got to face and keep your chin where it belongs.

With dearest love, always,

Daddy

P.S. In your telegram please say also *if* you are going to Norfolk, and *when*.

Dearest Scottie:

I'm going into a huddle on this script and probably won't be able to write you again at length before Vassar starts. I read the story in *College Bazaar* and was very pleased with it. You've put in some excellent new touches and its only fault is the jerkiness that goes with a story that has often been revised. Stories are best written in either one jump or three, according to the length. The three-jump story should be done on three successive days, then a day or so for revise and off she goes. This of course is the ideal —in many stories one strikes a snag that must be hacked at but, on the whole, stories that drag along or are terribly difficult (I mean a difficulty that comes from a poor conception and consequent faulty construction) never flow quite as well in the reading. However, I'm glad you published this one. It was nice to see your name.

About names, I don't quite know what to do. You calling yourself Frances Scott Fitzgerald does push me a little into the background. It calls attention to my being of my generation, which is not too good since I hope to have a big book out in a year. That is my only objection. There are three Van Dorens who write and people have long ago given up telling which is Rita, which is Mark, and which is Carl. I'm afraid that Frances Scott Fitzgerald is likely to lead to a certain confusion. What do you think?

You never told me why you stayed in New York so long—I rather gather somebody was married, possibly my Favorite Glamorist. All girls from 18 to 19 take the marriage of a friend as a heavy body blow but don't let it worry you, kid. Remember your old book, "Men Are Like Street Cars." Anyhow panic about such things is completely endemic to your age and has no basis in reality. God willing, you will have at least fifteen more years of being highly attractive to attractive men. And all this because you've never shaved your legs, plucked your eyebrows or criticized your father! . . . .

A last thought about other people's weddings—you don't have to be *right* about your objectives at the moment —only about your ways and means, learning Spanish, for instance, getting to know poetry. Honestly the ends will take care of themselves.

With dearest love,
Daddy

P.S. Also saw your account of a weekend at Yale, Harvard and Princeton. It was very colorful. Things don't seem to have changed much. Have you ever been to Cornell? Aw, tell me the truth, I won't dock your allowance. How much does *College Bazaar* pay you? If you remember, will you write me the name of a picture-frame store at Vassar and I'll have those Princeton etchings of Don Swann's framed for you before college starts.

SEPTEMBER 17, 1940

Dearest Scottina:

I hope they won't gun for you at college this year but from the tenor of the letter they sent about your work improving, I gather that they will. There was just a hint in it. You must try to realize their point of view and compromise with it. They feel they give you a lot and don't want you to use the place as simply a proving ground for individual egotisms—

—which, of course, is what you and I would like it to be. I went back to junior year with Princeton in my pocket and it took them four months to take it all away from me— stripped of every office and on probation—the phrase was "ineligible for extra-curricular activities." I was in the hospital besides.

Don't let it happen to you. It isn't necessary. *Start well* with your work—the old "initial impression." But if you took the whole play on your shoulders, as you threaten, you'll have to get straight B's to make them think you're doing *any* studying—can't you find some bright sophomores to do the work while you play the executive—bring them along "to inherit," so to speak? If any one man tried to do the Triangle he'd have a beautiful breakdown—it's a complex organization built up over years.

This is really such sensible advice—you've founded the club, you want to perpetuate it. All right—draw up an organization that will *really* divide the creative work, which

153

is to say the hard work. For you to write, cast, direct, bally-hoo and *manage*—and do any work or reading besides is an idiotic program. I know what effort is and I respect it but aren't you verging on the extravagant—you who pride yourself on your common sense?

When I set out to write a big novel at 21 it was ambitious and difficult—but when your mother started to catch up with Pavlova at 28 it was fantastic and impossible. Your trying to juggle this thing without a director or organization, with your *Harper's Bazaar* and your admirers and the games and parties, would lead to disaster. It doesn't take any prophet to make that observation—it just takes the most casual onlooker. No possible triumph is worth the loss of your health.

I could almost bet that you've done very little work on the play this summer—that it's uppermost on your mind now. That is just the beginning of the great confusion in which you will find yourself if you don't sit down *now* and decide what you can do and what you *can't*—and find others to delegate it to. Believe me—they'll let you do all the work—and heartily admire you—like they did me. They sent flowers too—but not to the footlights, where I expected them—only to the infirmary.

Your affectionate but somewhat concerned
Daddy

P.S. This is an advance on your next week's allowance as I know all your trips leave you penniless.

OCTOBER 5, 1940

Dearest Scottie:

Glad you liked *Death in Venice.* I don't see any connection between that and *Dorian Gray* except that they both
have an implied homosexuality. *Dorian Gray* is little more
than a somewhat highly charged fairy tale which stimulates
adolescents to intellectual activity at about seventeen (it did
the same for you as it did for me). Sometime you will re-
read it and see that it is essentially naive. It is in the lower
ragged edge of "literature," just as *Gone with the Wind* is
in the higher brackets of crowd entertainment. *Death in
Venice,* on the other hand, is a work of art, of the school
of Flaubert—yet not derivative at all. Wilde had two models
for *Dorian Gray:* Balzac's *Le Peau de Chagrin* and Huys-
mans' *A Rebours.*

After which literary lecture I can only sympathize with
the practically desolate state of Vassar and assure you that
many of those that have left will lament through their lives
that they didn't go on. In that connection, by the way,
aren't there many transfers from other colleges in junior
year? I should think after this past year everything would
indeed be anti-climax. You've had almost everything you
wanted—in Vassar, in Baltimore, and in general. But it's
rather lucky that in life we don't go on repeating. Certainly
you should have new objectives now—this of all years ought
to be the time of awakening for that nascent mind of yours.
Once one is caught up into the material world not one per-

son in ten thousand finds the time to form literary taste, to examine the validity of philosophic concepts for himself, or to form what, for lack of a better phrase, I might call the wise and tragic sense of life.

By this I mean the thing that lies behind all great careers, from Shakespeare's to Abraham Lincoln's, and as far back as there are books to read—the sense that life is essentially a cheat and its conditions are those of defeat, and that the redeeming things are not "happiness and pleasure" but the deeper satisfactions that come out of struggle. Having learned this in theory from the lives and conclusions of great men, you can get a hell of a lot more enjoyment out of whatever bright things come your way.

You speak of how good your generation is, but I think they share with every generation since the Civil War in America the sense of being somehow about to inherit the earth. You've heard me say before that I think the faces of most American women over thirty are relief maps of petulant and bewildered unhappiness.

Well, and fare thee well. You never answer the specific questions in my letters. You tell me about your courses in general, but not in particular. And that was an important question about your literary name—I'm against your using *two* names of mine, like in the *College Bazaar*.

With dearest love,
Daddy

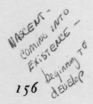

NASCENT—
coming into
existence—
beginning to
156 develop

1403 North Laurel Avenue
Hollywood, California

NOVEMBER 2, 1940

Dearest Scottina:

Listening to the Harvard-Princeton game on the radio with the old songs reminds me of the past that I lived a quarter of a century ago and that you are living now. I picture you as there though I don't know whether you are or not.

I remember once a long time ago I had a daughter who used to write me letters but now I don't know where she is or what she is doing, so I sit here listening to Puccini— "Someday she'll write (*Pigliano edda ciano*)."

With dearest love,
Daddy

Dearest Scottie:

I started Tom Wolfe's book on your recommendation.[1]
It seems better than *Time and the River*. He has a fine in-
clusive mind, can write like a streak, has a great deal of
emotion, though a lot of it is maudlin and inaccurate, but
his awful secret transpires at every crevice—he did not have
anything particular to say! The stuff about the GREAT
VITAL HEART OF AMERICA is just simply corny.

He recapitulates beautifully a great deal of what Walt
Whitman said and Dostoevski said and Nietzsche said and
Milton said, but he himself, unlike Joyce and T. S. Eliot
and Ernest Hemingway, has nothing really new to add. All
right—it's all a mess and it's too bad about the individual—
so what? Most writers line themselves up along a solid gold
bar like Ernest's courage, or Joseph Conrad's art, or D. H.
Lawrence's intense cohabitations, but Wolfe is too "smart"
for this and I mean smart in its most belittling and most
modern sense. Smart like Fadiman in *The New Yorker*,
smart like the critics whom he so pretends to despise. However, the book doesn't commit the cardinal sin: it doesn't
fail to live. But I'd like you to think sometime how and in
what way you think it is superior to such a piece of Zolaesque
naturalism as Maugham's *Of Human Bondage,* or if it is

---

[1] *You Can't Go Home Again.*

superior at all. Did you like the description of Max Perkins as "Foxhall?" I believe Max had mixed emotions.

I'm taking a day off from my novel to go to the dentist, the doctor, and my agent, to the latter in order to discuss picture business when and if I go back to it in February. And I have saved an hour to rush in where angels fear to tread. I don't know ———— and have had to piece him together from what you have told me and from a letter you showed me and so forth. But it sounds to me as if he had a perceptible dash of lavender. I know exactly what you mean about the Dwight Fiske attitude—sometimes the Harvard manner approaches that deceptively as a pose—but when a man is tired of life at 21 it indicates that he is rather tired of something in himself. One thing I'm sure of. There are plenty of absolutely first-rate men who will be within your range in the next two years. I remember that Lois Moran used to worry because all the attractive men she knew were married. She finally inverted it into the credo that if a man *wasn't* married and inaccessible, he wasn't a first-rate man. She gave herself a very bad time. The sea is still as full as ever of sharks, whales, trout and tuna. The real handicap for a girl like you would have been to have worn herself out emotionally at sixteen. I think we cut that by about two-thirds by keeping you comparatively busy in those two very crucial years. Life should be fun for you and there's plenty of time. All I care for is that you should marry someone who is not too much a part of the crowd.

Lanahan is wrong about your disposition. You take adversity very well, but you are utterly dependent on sleep. Your extraordinary performance out here two years ago was directly attributable to the fact that you hadn't slept since getting off the boat, if you slept on board of it! It amounts almost to an idiosyncracy in you and you should never make important decisions when you are extremely tired.

With dearest love,
Daddy

P.S. It's O.K. about the Xmas money but go slow. The phone rang after I finished this letter and the doctor after seeing my cardiogram has confined me to the house. So at this moment I *couldn't* go to the studios if I wanted to. Try to save your fare to Baltimore and back.

1403 North Laurel Avenue
Hollywood, California

DECEMBER 7, 1940

Dearest Scottie:

I'm sending the check you asked for next week. Will that be time enough? Also will send railroad fare, etc. I'm still in bed but managing to write and feeling a good deal better. It was a regular heart attack this time and I will simply have to take better care of myself. I've been living two floors up and will probably have to move, though not immediately.

It interests me what you are doing for Peaches. I should certainly think of nothing else but Peaches while you are writing it so it will be absolutely honest. But afterwards I would very much like to see a copy of it. Littauer, the editor of *Collier's*, came through here last week and liked your *New Yorker* piece very much. He might pay you more than almost anyone else. While I'm on the subject, remember that Harold Ober's advice is only good up to a point. He is "the average reader" and about one third of the stories that I sold to *The Saturday Evening Post* were stories which he did not think they would buy. Like all agents, he is clogged with too much of the kind of reading trained to smell the money in the page—so I should never ask his advice on any literary matter, though of course in other regards he is an excellent agent.

My novel is something of a mystery, I hope. I think it's a pretty good rule not to tell what a thing is about until it's finished. If you do you always seem to lose some of it. It never quite belongs to you so much again.

Your Xmas plans seem O.K. to me.

With dearest love,
[*Daddy*]

Dearest Scottie:

There has reached you by this time, I hope, a little coat. It was an almost never-worn coat of Sheilah's that she wanted to send you. It seemed very nice to me—it may fill out your rather thin wardrobe. Frances Kroll's father is a furrier and he remade it *without charge!*

So you must *at once please* write the following letters:

(1) To Sheilah, not stressing Mr. Kroll's contribution.
(2) To Frances, praising the style.
(3) To me (in the course of things) in such a way that I can show the letter to *Sheilah* who will certainly ask me if you liked the coat.

You make things easier for me if you write these letters promptly. A giver gets no pleasure in a letter acknowledging a gift three weeks' late even though it crawls with apologies —you will have stolen pleasure from one who has tried to give it to you. (Ecclesiastes Fitzgerald)

Lastly, drum up some story for Alabama that you bought the coat from some girl. Don't say it came through me.

For the rest, I am still in bed—this time the result of twenty-five years of cigarettes. You have got two beautiful bad examples for parents. Just do everything we didn't do and you will be perfectly safe. But be sweet to your mother

163

at Xmas despite her early Chaldean rune-worship which she will undoubtedly inflict on you at Xmas. Her letters are tragically brilliant on all matters except those of central importance. How strange to have failed as a social creature— even criminals do not fail that way—they are the law's "Loyal Opposition," so to speak. But the insane are always mere guests on earth, eternal strangers carrying around broken decalogues that they cannot read.

I am still not through Tom Wolfe's novel and can't finally report it but the story of the fire is magnificent. Only I'm afraid that after the grand character-planting nothing is going to come of it all. The picture of "Amy Carleton" (Emily Davies Vanderbilt who used to come to our apartment in Paris—do you remember?), with the cracked grey eyes and the exactly reproduced speech, is just simply perfect. She tried hard to make Tom—*sans succès*—and finally ended by her own hand in Montana in 1934 in a lonely ranch house. The portrait of Mrs. Jack is grand too. I believe her absolutely.

With dearest love,
Daddy

P.S. In the name of Somerset Maugham, the *letter!*

All good writing is *swimming under water* and holding your breath.

The conclusion is: it will not win you either financial independence or immortality. But you will be wise to publish it, if you can—if for no gain and only in a college magazine. It will give you a sense of your own literary existence, and put you in touch with others trying the same thing. In a literary way I cannot help you beyond a point. I might say that I don't think anyone can write succinct prose unless they have at least tried and failed to write a good iambic pentameter sonnet, and read Browning's short dramatic poems, etc.—but that was my personal approach to prose. Yours may be different, as Ernest Hemingway's was. But I wouldn't have written this long letter unless I distinguished, underneath the sing-song lilt of your narrative, some traces of a true rhythm that is ear-marked Scottina. There is as yet no honesty—the reader will say "so what?" But when in a freak moment you will want to give the low-down, not the scandal, not the merely *reported* but the *profound* essence of what happened at a prom or after it, perhaps that honesty will come to you—and then you will understand how it is possible to make even a forlorn Laplander *feel* the importance of a trip to Cartier's!

The first thing I ever sold was a piece of verse to *Poet Lore* when I was twenty.

I shall somehow manage not to appear in a taxi-cab on Thanksgiving and thus disgrace you before all those "nice" girls. Isn't it somewhat old-fashioned to describe girls in expensive backgrounds as "nice?" I will bet two-thirds of the girls at Miss Walker's school have at least one grandparent that peddled old leather in the slums of New York, Chicago or London, and if I thought you were accepting the standards of the cosmopolitan rich, I would much rather have you in a southern school, where scholastic standards are not so high and the word "nice" is not debased to such a ludicrous extent. I have seen the whole racket, and if there is any more disastrous road than that from Park Avenue to the Rue de la Paix and back again, I don't know it.

They are homeless people, ashamed of being American, unable to master the culture of another country; ashamed, usually, of their husbands, wives, grandparents, and unable to bring up descendants of whom they could be proud, even if they had the nerve to bear them, ashamed of each other yet leaning on each other's weakness, a menace to the social order in which they live—oh, why should I go on? You know how I feel about such things. If I come up and find you gone Park Avenue, you will have to explain me away as a Georgia cracker or a Chicago killer. God help Park Avenue.

Madame Curie progresses and it is a relief to be working on something that the censors have nothing against. It will be a comparatively quiet picture—as was *The Barretts of Wimpole Street*, but the more I read about the woman the more I think about her as one of the most admirable people of our time. I hope we can get a little of that into the story.

You must have some politeness toward ideas. You can neither cut through, nor challenge nor beat the fact that there is an organized movement over the world before which you and I as individuals are less than the dust. Sometime when you feel very brave and defiant and haven't been invited to one particular college function, read the terrible chapter in *Das Kapital* on "The Working Day," and see if you are ever quite the same.

So many writers, Conrad for instance, have been aided by being brought up in a métier utterly unrelated to literature. It gives an abundance of material and, more important, an attitude from which to view the world. So much writing nowadays suffers both from lack of an attitude and from sheer lack of any material, save what is accumulated in a purely social life. The world, as a rule, does not live on beaches and in country clubs.

INDEX